WOMEN IN THE MILITARY

Other books in the At Issue series:

WOMEN
IN THE
MILITARY

James Haley, *Book Editor*

Bruce Glassman, *Vice President*
Bonnie Szumski, *Publisher*
Helen Cothran, *Managing Editor*

OPPOSING
VIEWPOINTS®
SERIES

GREENHAVEN
PRESS®

THOMSON
———— ✦ ————™
GALE

San Diego • Detroit • New York • San Francisco • Cleveland
New Haven, Conn. • Waterville, Maine • London • Munich

LIBRARY OF CONGRESS CATALOGING-IN-PUBLICATION DATA
Women in the military / James Haley, book editor.
p. cm. — (At issue)
Includes bibliographical references and index.
ISBN 0-7377-2299-1 (pbk. : alk. paper) — ISBN 0-7377-2298-3 (lib. : alk. paper)
1. United States—Armed Forces—Women. I. Haley, James, 1968– . II. At issue (San Diego, Calif.)
UB418.W65W6724 2004
355'.0082'0973—dc22   2003064685

Printed in the United States of America

Contents

Introduction

On March 23, 2003, during the third full day of the U.S. invasion of Iraq, an army convoy carrying cooks, mechanics, and support personnel was ambushed by Iraq soldiers in the city of Nasiriya. Private Jessica Lynch, a supply clerk, suffered two broken legs and a head injury in the attack before being captured by Iraqi soldiers. She was taken to a hospital where she was interrogated and physically abused by Iraqi military officers, who, according to hospital staff, intended to have her executed. Lynch was rescued by American forces on April 1 after an Iraqi, concerned about her mistreatment at the hospital, made his way to a U.S. Marine camp and provided information about where Lynch was being held. Her bravery in the face of brutality was widely reported in the media and highlighted the U.S. military's less restrictive service policies that have placed more women inside dangerous combat zones. In fact, close to 90 percent of military jobs are now open to the nearly two hundred thousand women—16 percent of total U.S. military personnel—who currently serve in the armed forces. Women fly helicopters and fighter jets, serve on combat ships, and command military police units.

Women are still not permitted to serve in units that engage in direct ground combat with the enemy, however. Direct ground combat is defined by Congress as "engaging an enemy on the ground with individual or crew-served weapons, while being exposed to hostile fire and to a high probability of direct physical contact with the hostile force's personnel." The definition precludes women from serving in positions such as the infantry, artillery, and special operations.

The mental and physical toughness exhibited by Lynch during her captivity prompted a renewed debate over whether the military is justified in continuing to exclude women from ground combat positions. Feminists and media pundits made Lynch a "poster girl" for the professionalism women have demonstrated in the heat of battle. Proponents of women in combat argue that the combat restriction limits the career advancement of qualified servicewomen, who need combat experience to move up the chain of military command. As the capture of Lynch demonstrates, the changing nature of modern warfare has challenged the notion that "safe" places exist on the battlefield. Explains J. Michael Brower, a program specialist at the U.S. Department of Justice, "Since combat finds women in today's frontlineless combat environment, the only useful purpose [ground combat] restrictions serve is to deprive females of rising to the most operationally meaningful positions." Meanwhile, opponents remain steadfast in their contention that the gender-integration of the infantry and other ground combat units would significantly undermine the capability and readiness of the U.S. military.

In reaching this final barrier, women have achieved a long and distinguished record of service for the United States, participating in every major U.S. conflict since the Revolutionary War. During World War II, more than three hundred thousand women were recruited into temporary branches of the military such as the WAACs (Women's Army Auxiliary Corps) and the Navy's WAVES (Women Accepted for Voluntary Emergency Service). In 1948, Congress passed the Armed Forces Women's Integration Act which, as Lorry M. Fenner, a lieutenant colonel in the Air Force explains, "gave women permanent regular status [and] . . . encouraged them to aspire to 'careers,' [although] restrictive service policies largely discouraged them from doing so." The act also limited women to no more than 2 percent of the enlisted ranks, a number that would hold steady for decades.

In the early 1970s, important changes—both cultural and institutional—took root that made the U.S. military more favorable to the recruitment and broader participation of women. In 1973, Congress and President Richard Nixon eliminated the unpopular military draft, which had been in effect during the long Vietnam War (1964–1975). The draft was replaced with the All-Volunteer Force (AVF), making the armed forces dependent on the recruitment of volunteers. The shift to the AVF coincided with the height of the women's movement and women's struggle for equal rights in the workplace. Feminists targeted the military as a bastion of sexism that offered unequal pay and limited career opportunities to servicewomen. Bowing to the pressure of the women's movement and increasingly dependent on attracting female recruits, branches of the armed forces opened more positions to women and paid them salaries comparable to those paid men. As a result, the numbers of enlisted women grew considerably throughout the 1970s and 1980s.

In 1975, the rapid pace of cultural change led Congress to force America's military service academies—the U.S. Military Academy (West Point), the Naval Academy, and the Air Force Academy—to admit women beginning with the class of 1976. According to Lance Janda in *A Soldier and a Woman: Sexual Integration in the Military*, the elite service academies were "created by Congress . . . so that every branch of the armed forces would benefit from having an institution dedicated solely to producing career officers." Women now had access to the training that would significantly advance their military careers and move them far closer to serving in the frontlines of combat. Janda maintains that "the admission of women [to the service academies] was part of a larger social revolution which sought to redefine the roles women, and ultimately men could play in American culture. . . . [Congress] took a dramatic step towards sending women into combat and fundamentally altering their roles within the military."

The effect of these changes on women's participation in the military became evident during the 1990–1991 Persian Gulf War, also known as Operation Desert Storm, fought to end the Iraqi occupation of neighboring Kuwait. More than forty thousand women were deployed in the war, many of whom served directly in the battle zone. According to William B. Breuer, author of *War and American Women: Heroism, Deeds, and Controversy*, "Never had females served in such a wide spectrum of tasks as they would in the Persian Gulf. . . . Women were involved as truck drivers, intelligence specialists, communications experts, flight controllers, cargo handlers, and other tasks." Thirteen servicewomen were killed and others were wounded or taken prisoner; however, none was technically classified as a "combat" soldier. In the aftermath of the war, some observers asserted that women had "finally proved themselves and merited complete equality" by the lifting of all remaining combat restrictions, according to Lorry M. Fenner, a lieutenant colonel in the Air Force. In 1993, opportunities for women were expanded by Defense Secretary Les Aspin, although not to the extent envisioned by feminists. Asserting that "we know from Operation Desert Storm that women can stand up to the most demanding environments," Aspin instructed that all except for direct ground combat positions be opened to women. This change gave women the opportunity to serve in combat planes and ships and other military units that have a high probability of engaging in combat.

In 2003, with the latest deployment of thousands of women to Iraq, the debate on lifting the direct ground combat barrier centers around the "cohesion" of combat units and whether women will disrupt unit cohesion. Cohesion is generally described as the factors that enable soldiers to work together for the common good within the high-pressure environment of combat. The group bonding achieved through complete trust in the physical and mental capabilities of other unit members is one factor that contributes to cohesion. Another cohesive factor is the recognition that personal relationships within the group should never take precedence over the performance of the group as a whole.

To critics of gender-integration, women possess physical and biological handicaps that will damage the cohesion of combat units. Skeptics contend that women are not as physically strong as men, creating a sense of wariness in male soldiers that a woman can be relied upon to perform essential functions on the battlefield. For example, it may take two women to do the job of one man, or a woman may lack the strength to carry a wounded soldier out of harm's way. Says Stephanie Gutmann, author of *The Kinder, Gentler Military*, "What happens when you try to integrate into a cohesive whole two populations with radically different bodies? In the elemental, unremittingly physical world of the soldier, sex differences . . . stand out in high relief. . . . [The female soldier] is, on average, about five inches shorter than the male soldier, has half the upper body strength, lower aerobic capacity and 37 percent less muscle mass."

Menstruation and pregnancy are also viewed as impeding unit cohesion. Men can go for weeks, even months, without showering while women must attend to feminine hygiene needs in an unsanitary environment of zero privacy. In addition, current military policy does not punish women who become pregnant but simply removes them from active duty. Critics fear that women will use pregnancy as a way to get out of combat service, disrupting the level of bonding and cohesion that a combat unit has achieved.

Perhaps most important is the concern that men will inevitably find themselves attracted to the opposite sex and will compete for the attentions of women. This raises the specter of personal relationships and jealousy corroding the cohesion of the unit. Argues Anna Simons, author of *The Company They Keep: Life Inside the U.S. Army Special Forces*, "The interest in women that serves as a sure-fire bond among [male-only combat units] becomes a cleaver dividing them as soon as women are present. . . . Benign posturing turns into serious competition. . . . In the wake of rivalry come envy, frustration, impatience, disgust. Women cannot help but rearrange the team's comfort zone." In Simons's view, whether intentional or not, women will plant the seeds of mistrust among the men in a unit.

Some military personnel do not view the problems described above as insurmountable. U.S. Army Majors Kim Field and John Nagl, who have conducted research into gender-integrating combat units, maintain that adopting several policy changes will prevent most, if not all, of the problems associated with women and unit cohesion. For one, they assert that an important step in reassuring male soldiers of the physical competence of women in combat units is to impose gender-blind physical fitness testing. This change would eliminate lower physical fitness requirements for women, which have driven complaints that a double standard exists regarding women's physical strength. Instead, gender-blind physical-fitness testing would ensure that "only those individuals who meet the standards required to accomplish the task inherent in that military specialty—male or female—would be allowed to serve in that specialty," according to Field and Nagl. The problem of pregnancy disrupting unit cohesion could also be reduced. The two researchers suggest that "all women receive and adhere to a birth control regime as part of the 'immunizations' required for a deployment. . . . If women are aware of a birth control requirement before enlisting . . . there should be no problem." Finally, Field and Nagl concede that sexual attraction may pose a threat to unit cohesion, but "anecdotal evidence abounds of [romantic] relationships among soldiers in highly successful combat support units."

Unquestionably, women are serving closer than ever before to the direct lines of combat. And so far, no great public outcry has demanded a restructuring of the military's deployment of women. In fact, 67 percent of Americans polled by *Time* magazine in 1997 supported the statement that women should be allowed to serve in combat roles. Given the enormous strides women have made professionally in the military over the past thirty years, it seems likely that branches of the armed services will provide women with the opportunity to serve in gender-integrated combats units, at least on an experimental basis. To Air Force lieutenant Colonel Lorry M. Fenner, removing the combat barrier will confer the complete rights of citizenship to women, finally granting them access to the full spectrum of leadership opportunities and status available to military men. Asks Fenner, "[The United States] acts as if military service (at least for men) confers some added status or earned privilege in our society. How can we then bar anyone from [combat] service and continue to consider them to be citizens?" Yet, equating combat experience with full citizenship runs the risk of excessively valorizing military service and could prove harmful to a democratic society. Explains feminist researcher Marie deYoung, "Demanding military service as a prerequisite to special benefits and leadership positions in American society can only . . . undermine the rights of . . . noncombatants in society by privileging warrior status for preferential treatment, pay, advancement, and political power." Many women will be made to feel like second-class citizens if they are not capable of the "brute force" necessary for combat, in deYoung's opinion. Ultimately, perhaps, the debate over women in combat may have less to do with citizenship rights, democratic ideals, and gender equality than whether the military can continue to provide the best possible defense for the nation—its foremost mission—with gender-integrated combat units. Only by giving servicewomen a chance to prove themselves in combat units will the military determine if its mission has been compromised. This debate is further examined in *Women in the Military: At Issue*. Other issues debated and discussed include registering women for the service draft and the efficacy of gender-integrated basic training.

1

Women Lack the Physical Strength to Be Soldiers

Brian Mitchell

Brian Mitchell is the author of Women in the Military: Flirting with Disaster, *from which the following viewpoint is excerpted.*

Contrary to the notion that technology has alleviated the need for physical strength in the military, the limited physical strength of servicewomen has a direct impact on their ability to perform assigned duties. Tests of men and women have shown that on average, women possess only 80 percent the overall strength of men, and servicewomen find many workday duties beyond their physical capabilities. The physical limitations of women—abetted by relaxed standards for height, weight, and reach—have degraded the ability of gender-integrated units to accomplish their missions, with dangerous and, in some situations, life-threatening consequences.

For many years, the party line in Washington was that all was well with women in the military, that with the exception of a few minor annoyances to be dispelled by the magic wand of policy, sexual integration was proceeding smoothly without degrading military readiness. Women were "an integral part" of the nation's defense, and they can do the job "as well as if not better" than their male comrades, said responsible officials.

Doubting the performance of women

The proof, they said, was in the women's consistently faster rate of promotion. In the spring of 1987, the Army promoted 33 percent of eligible women to the rank of E-7 [Sergeant First Class] but only 16 percent of eligible men. Throughout the services, women are promoted with less time-in-service than men to every grade from E-2 [Private] to O-7. Female officers are promoted to rear admiral and brigadier general (O-7) fives years earlier than men, on average, and enlisted women to senior NCO [Corporal] or chief petty officer rank (E-7) two to four years earlier than enlisted men.

But there are several reasons for doubting the significance of promotion comparisons. Higher rates of attrition and lower rates of retention trim much of the dead wood from the women's ranks. In the past, those who survived until retirement were intensely dedicated women who forsook marriage and family for the sake of their careers. Today less dedicated women are favored by promotion systems that emphasize education, test scores, and personal appearance—areas where women tend to outdo men. Moreover, promotions are centrally controlled and therefore not immune from manipulation. The services not only exert considerable pressure to safeguard the advancement of women; they use rigid quotas to guarantee that women succeed.

The assertion that women in general are performing as well as or better than men has by no means been proven. No doubt some women outperform some men, but the many good servicewomen who excel at their jobs do not compensate the services for the problems that women overall have caused them, problems that have been known for many years, but which are religiously ignored for political reasons.

Physical limitations and technology

The general lack of physical strength among servicewomen bears directly upon their ability to perform assigned duties. Yet the notion that technology has alleviated the need for physical strength is almost universally accepted. Say the words "modern warfare" and the minds of many Americans fill with images of control consoles and video displays. "There's an awful lot of button-pushing going on out there," says a reporter for *Time* magazine who thinks the physical demands of the military have been exaggerated.

There is, however, no evidence that technology has in fact reduced the need for physical strength and endurance among military men and women. Endurance has only increased in importance; operations are now conducted around the clock and throughout the year, whereas they were once limited to the daytime in seasonable weather. Many modern military jobs still require more physical strength than most women possess. Technology has not provided the Air Force with automatic litter-loaders to move wounded soldiers onto MEDEVAC aircraft, a task women are unable to do, nor of sorting artillery rounds by hand. What technology has done is to make service members able to do more, thereby making more for them to do. Many of the buttons that need pushing are attached to large pieces of equipment that must be hauled in haste back and forth across the battlefield.

The assertion that [military] women . . . are performing as well as or better than men has by no means been proven.

Women's physical advantages are that they are less susceptible to altitude sickness and, normally, have a greater tolerance of cold temperatures due to their extra body fat. But by all other measures, men have enormous advantages physically. The average female Army recruit is 4.8 inches shorter, 31.7 pounds lighter, has 37.4 fewer pounds of muscle, and

5.7 more pounds of fat than the average male recruit. She has only 55 percent of the upper-body strength and 72 percent of the lower-body strength of the average male. She is also at a significant disadvantage when performing aerobic activities such as marching with heavy loads and working in the heat, since fat mass is inversely related to aerobic capacity and heat tolerance. Her lighter frame, moreover, makes her more likely to suffer injuries due to physical exertion. An Army study of 124 men and 186 women done in 1988 found that women are more than twice as likely to suffer leg injuries and nearly five times as likely to suffer fractures as men. Women were, consequently, less available for duty.

The gap in physical abilities

There is without doubt a significant gap between the physical abilities of men and women. Tests of men and women entering the West Point [class of 1980 found that, on average, the upper-body strength of women was 56 percent the strength of men, their leg strength 80 percent, and their gripping strength 69 percent. Even when height was kept constant, women possessed only 80 percent of the overall strength of men. After eight weeks of intensive training, male plebes demonstrated 32 percent more power in the lower body and performed 48 percent more work at the leg press than female plebes. At the bench press, the men demonstrated 270 percent more power and performed an extraordinary 473 percent more work than the women.

Little wonder that servicewomen should find so many workaday duties beyond their ability. Even in the modern Air Force, routine tasks are often too much for them. The Government Accounting Office (GAO) found that 62 of 97 female aircraft mechanics could not perform required tasks such as changing aircraft tires and brakes, removing batteries and crew seats, closing drag chute doors, breaking torque on bolts, and lifting heavy stands. Female missile mechanics often lacked the strength and physical confidence to harness and move warheads and to maneuver large pieces of machinery. Some had trouble carrying their own tool boxes.

In the late 1970s the Air Force began screening recruits using the "X-Factor" strength indicator, but Army researchers found that the screening had degenerated in practice into a meaningless question-and-answer drill. Had the X-Factor actually kept women out of jobs for which they were unfit, it would have gone the way of the Army's MEPSCAT. The very presence of women in the ranks was made possible only by lowering or eliminating physical standards. When the services found that weight standards for recruits excluded 22 percent of potential female recruits but only 3 percent of potential male recruits, the standards were revised to resemble the insurance industry's standards, excluding 7.3 percent of women and 5.8 percent of men. A five-foot-six-inch female may now enlist in the Army weighing a hefty 165 lbs. All of the services have double standards for men and women on all the events of their regular physical fitness tests. Young male marines must perform at least three pull-ups to pass the test, but women marines must only hang from the bar with arms flexed for sixteen seconds. In the Anny Army, the youngest women are given an extra three minutes to complete a two-mile run. All of the services require men to perform more situps than women, though the Army just pledged to change this.

To justify the double standard, the American military abandoned the worldwide consensus of the purpose for physical training in the military—that soldiers should be tougher, faster, stronger, and more physically able than the rest of the populace. The U.S. military prefers weak but healthy people because they are cheaper in the long run. Physical training is meant to "ensure a minimum level of fitness, not to delineate any measure of job-related productivity," thus "the premise that men 'do more' because they must achieve higher physical fitness standards is not a valid one."

Degrading mission accomplishment

Of course, on the job, men actually do more to make up for the limitations of their female coworkers. As long as there are enough men around, commanders can pretend that women have not degraded a unit's ability to accomplish its mission. But as their number increased, the concentration of women in some support units began to threaten mission accomplishment. Naval Air Station Adak in the Aleutian Islands of Alaska boasted a fire department that was 76 percent female. The women were issued special, lighter fire-fighting equipment, and portions of the International Fire Service Association manuals were rewritten to cover how the women should cope with physically demanding tasks. But because the women were still unable to open and close fire hydrants, connect large diameter hoses, advance hose lines, and control nozzles, the department was forced to assign five women to engine companies that normally required only four men— a 25 percent increase in personnel to do the same job.

Aboard ship, the entire crew is charged with fire-fighting and rescue duties, and here the substitution of women for men can have deadly consequences. A 1981 Navy study found female recruits woefully unable to perform five common damage-control tasks: carrying stretchers up and down ladders and across level surfaces, moving and starting emergency pumps, turning engine bolts, and directing fire hoses. Test results are shown in Table 1.

Table 1. Number of Recruits Not Capable of Performing Damage-Control Tasks				
Task	# of Women before training	# of Women after training	# of Men before training	# of Men after training
Stretcher carry level	63	38	0	0
Stretcher carry up/ down ladder	94	88	0	0
Fire hose	19	16	0	0
P250 pump, carry down	99	99	9	4
P250 pump, carry up	73	52	0	0
P250 pump, start pump	90	75	0	0
Remove SSTG pump	99	99	0	0
Torque engine bolt	78	47	0	0

The implications were ominous. "Unless the Navy has the luxury of customizing damage control assignments based upon the capabilities of individual sailors, the lack of physical strength among female soldiers can only decrease the survivability of Navy vessels," wrote Dr. Paul Davis, an exercise physiologist, in an article for *Navy Times*. "Seen in this light, the Navy's recent enthusiasm for putting more and more women aboard ship makes little sense, unless the Navy doesn't mind sacrificing survivability (and possibly the lives of its sailors) for the sake of enhancing opportunities for women."

Army experts who were not personally involved in the WITA study have innocently compared a soldier's need for strength to an athlete's, without considering the implications for women. According to Major James Wright, chief of the Exercise Science Branch of the U.S. Army Fitness School:

> Upper-body strength is an important component of virtually every Army task. There are still hundreds of manual-type tasks which require strength. There will always be a lot of setting up and tearing down of equipment when units go to the field. In fact, several studies show that the lack of upper-body strength is actually a limiting factor for our overall military readiness.

Navy Lieutenant Ed Marcinik, an exercise physiologist working with the Naval Health and Physical Readiness Program, agree:

> There are general shipboard tasks that every sailor must perform, all requiring upper-body strength: extricating injured personnel, controlling fire hose nozzles, handling stores, and opening and securing watertight hatches, doors, and scuttles.

Marcinik says that fully 84 percent of all shipboard duties involve heavy lifting, carrying, or pulling. Four ratings (boatswain's mate, gunner's mate, hull technician, and machinist's mate) are among the most physically demanding jobs in the military.

Devaluing physical prowess

Before the Navy became so sensitive to the feelings of women, it developed a program of shipboard weight training called SPARTEN, or Scientific Program of Aerobic and Resistance Training Exercise in the Navy. One part of SPARTEN involved the installation of nautilus equipment on ships like the battleship *New Jersey*.

To military women, however, such emphasis on physical strength is anathema. When men in the military are encouraged to think that being strong and quick is good, the professional reputation of military women suffers. Because the services are committed to protect and advance women as equals, they devalue physical prowess as a professional virtue, which is why programs like SPARTEN are only marginally effective.

Apart from the lack of strength and speed, the smaller size and different shape of women has caused innumerable problems solved only by a boom in special clothing and equipment. The defense inventory has burgeoned with end-items specially designed for both sexes or women only, including smaller everything from snowshoes to flight suits: smaller wire-cutters, longer wrenches, lighter firefighters' helmets, specially cut boots; special helicopter seats because women complained of back pain; flak vests to accommodate female breasts; gas-masks to fit softer, smaller, less bony faces; and a disposable cardboard tube to enable female soldiers to urinate in the field without dropping their trousers (developed but not adopted). In the interest of uniformity and standardization, the Army has tried to develop clothing that will fit both men and women with minimum variation, but the unsightly compromises fit neither sex well.

Many modern military jobs still require more physical strength than most women possess.

A more serious result of the differences of shape and size is the relaxation of anthropometric standards devised to fit the operator to the equipment. The services have always been willing to relax standards for height, weight, and reach in order to admit women to special programs and training. None of the first women to undergo Navy flight training in 1975 satisfied the Navy's own stringent standards that excluded many men. In 1983, to enhance pilot safety and aircraft performance, the Navy tightened requirements for sitting height, leg length, buttock-to-knee length, and functional reach, but when female aviators complained that only a quarter of them would qualify, the Navy backed off.

Anthropometric differences also affect the design of new systems and equipment with potentially serious consequences. There is no such thing as a one-size-fits-all high-performance jet fighter. For the safety of the pilot and for the performance of the aircraft, cockpits are made to be tight fits. When designers introduce a 25 percent variable in the size of the pilot, something must give.

Weaker soldiers, greater risks

The need to accommodate smaller, weaker soldiers played a part in the Army's decision to replace the M1911 .45 caliber Colt pistol with the 9mm Beretta. The best buy the Army ever made, the .45 automatic was designed to stop a drug-crazed Moro warrior dead in his tracks. It served all of the services well in every war since World War I, but lately fell victim to complaints that it was difficult to use effectively because it was unwieldy and heavy—so heavy that female military policemen were issued .38 caliber revolvers instead.

The Army insists that the .45's ineffectiveness and the need for standardization within North Atlantic Treaty Organization (NATO), not the inability of women to use it, motivated the change, but this raises the question of why the Army is not also considering a replacement for the M16 rifle. Since its adoption, the M16 has been criticized by experienced soldiers as being mechanically unreliable, lacking in stopping power, ineffective at long ranges, and too fragile for combat use. The NATO standard rifle caliber is 7.65mm, but the M16 is a 5.56mm rifle and United

States is the only country in NATO to use it. But any 7.65mm alternative weighs many pounds more than the M16, posing a significant problem for female soldiers. And in almost every instance the good of equal opportunity takes precedence over the good of the service.

Ultimately, of course, the lack of physical strength among women will directly degrade the ability of units to fight and survive on the modern battlefield, inevitably resulting in a greater loss of life and a greater risk of defeat.

2

Properly Trained Servicewomen Can Overcome Physical Shortcomings

Rosemarie Skaine

Rosemarie Skaine is the author of Women at War: Gender Issues of Americans in Combat, *from which the following viewpoint is excerpted.*

Concerns that servicewomen lag behind men in physical strength are misplaced. Research demonstrates that technical skill, intelligence, and training are more important in today's technologically advanced military than sheer physical strength. Nevertheless, military institutions have not altered their physical readiness requirements to accommodate women except where absolutely necessary. In addition, a 1995 military study indicates that the majority of women can develop the strength required for traditional male military duties if trained correctly. All soldiers—whether male or female—should have to meet the full scope of physical requirements to be allowed in direct combat-related positions. Such a policy will preclude accusations that women are not qualified to be soldiers.

A discussion of ability in the military almost always provokes questions about whether women can "measure up" to some specific standard in some specific test whose consequence will be apparent at some specific time. The congressional hearings of 1993 and 1994 and the 1993 Presidential Commission's report [*Report to the President: Women in Combat*] are filled with effective argumentation to fit any position and to support any argument. They include statements that it is not physical characteristics but cohesion and absolute trust that are more important. The Presidential Commission recommended that the services should retain gender-specific physical fitness tests and standards to promote the highest level of fitness and wellness in the armed forces. The Commission was more divided, however, when it discussed occupational physical requirements, basic training standards, and precommissioning standards. It voted 14-0 that the services should adopt gender-neutral muscular strength and endurance and cardiovascular requirements for those specialties for which they are relevant. The purpose of the 1994 hearing of the Military Forces and Personnel Subcommittee of the House Committee on Armed Services, titled Assignment of Army and Marine Corps Women Under the New Definition of Ground Combat, was to evaluate the impact of changes in assignment policy for women on the constitutionality of an all-male military selective service and the need to establish gender-neutral physical performance standards for military positions being opened up for both sexes. What do all of these multitudes of tests and positions mean? Most interviewees say, "Assign a military position on the basis of a person's qualifications, not gender." As Captain Rosemary Mariner, U.S. Navy (USN) has said, "A Soldier Is a Soldier." Unfortunately, if physical qualifications are approached on the basis of gender, then qualifications will not have to be closely examined. Thus, rather than present every physical test that I can find and present every single argument for or against a certain aspect of physical testing, I have chosen to present some reasoning to support Captain Mariner's concept, "A Soldier Is a Soldier."

Gender and strength, stamina, and other biological differences

Division of labor may have been useful in earlier times, but it is less so now. Technology, as Mady Segal points out [in the 1995 article "Women's Military Roles Cross-Nationally; Past, Present, and Future"], has decreased the importance of physical strength and reproduction. How society deals with gender differences is very important. Women's roles in the military are a cultural interpretation of gender. Cultures can stress gender equality or gender differences, and stressing either will have an effect on the military woman's role. Segal maintains, "The greater the emphasis on ascription by gender (and thereby the less the emphasis on individual differences), the more limited women's military role."

It is more important now to have superior technical skill, intelligence, and training [in the military than physical strength].

Lieutenant Michael J. Frevola, an attorney who is a member of the U.S. Naval Reserve, agrees with Segal that with the advent of modern weaponry, Congress's concerns that women will be overpowered are misplaced. It is more important now to have superior technical skill, intelligence, and training. Even the Army and Marine Corps are mechanized in some fashion and possess automatic and lightweight weaponry. Some specialties such as Special Forces still require uncommon physical strength, but their numbers are small and their requirements prohibit an "overwhelming majority of men and women from becoming members." Frevola's research shows, however, that the Department of Defense no longer supports the idea that women cannot fill the position of a front-line infantryman successfully. According to Frevola, military sources have said that military institutions have not altered their physical readiness requirements to accommodate women except where absolutely necessary. The Navy and Marine Corps acknowledge that a service member who successfully completes basic training can fill any line position, but in 1996 the Army and Air Force still utilize strength testing for same jobs. Frevola believes there is always a "gender overlap"—the strongest and largest women will be stronger and larger than the smallest men eligible for combat duty. If strength requirements for graduating basic training for men and women were the same, the weakest women in the ranks would not be weaker than the weakest man and thus any worse off than some of her fellow male soldiers. Strength requirements should be decided by position, he concludes, and not by gender.

Brigadier General Margaret A. Brewer, U.S. Marine Corps (USMC) (Retired), believes that military women could appropriately be assigned to all occupational fields except the direct ground combat specialties. These specialties generally require a high degree of physical strength. She adds, "If, at some future time, a decision is made to assign women to direct ground combat specialties then valid definitive performance standards should be established for men and women. The establishment of such physical strength standards would help to ensure that anyone, male or female, who does not meet the standards would not be assigned to that combat specialty."

Ability of women to carry their weight

Before the Army froze the recruiting of women at about nine percent during the Ronald Reagan presidential administration, General Edward C. Meyer, Army Chief of Staff during the Jimmy Carter presidential administration, established the Women in the Army Policy Review Group (WITA) which was charged with reviewing the issues involved and formulating policy. The direct combat definition became official, and the issue of physical capabilities surfaced. WITA established physical strength requirements for each military occupation specialty (MOS). The General Accounting Office (GAO) also recommended gender-free strength testing of potential recruits. WITA agreed, saying, "The Army cannot be assured of accomplishing the ground combat mission if women are randomly accessed into positions with physically demanding tasks exceeding their capabilities." The Air Force developed similar tests. A test to measure strength and endurance, MEPSCAT (Military Enlistment Physical Strength Capacity Test), was developed but never implemented. In 1985 the Air Force dismissed WITA's findings "because there was no proof that those who lacked the strength to perform their assigned tasks actually degraded unit effectiveness."

Major Paul Christopher, U.S. Army (USA), maintains that if assignments to combat units are restricted based on physical standards, those standards must be applied equally to both sexes. To apply them only to women is unreasonable and discriminatory, he adds. He rejects the arguments that try to exclude women from combat based on an alleged physical difference.

Physical fitness tests, referred to as PT tests, determine individual physical fitness, not qualification, for combat readiness, says Major Lillian A. Pfluke. Gender and age norming is the only way to measure physical fitness accurately. "This is NOT to say that the physical qualifying standards for jobs should be gender or aged normed," clarifies Pfluke. Using physical fitness tests as a reason to exclude women from jobs that they are qualified for is a wrong use of the tests, and these tests can sometimes affect morale. Pfluke proposes more education within the services as to the true purpose of these tests.

Some observers argue that certain women would be strong enough to be in the infantry, but they would be such a minority that their numbers in the infantry would not reach critical mass, in the psychological sense. In 1993 the Canadian infantry found that when they opened to women, they got one volunteer. She was a very lonely infantry person Lieutenant General Thomas P. Carney, Deputy Chief of Staff for Personnel, USA, says that for reasons of unit cohesion and other issues he doesn't see the Army voluntarily or involuntarily placing women into infantry roles. The question we have to ask Carney and others who hold similar positions is, do we reach critical mass of needed numbers with all men? Another argument posed is that men are more aggressive. But as Helen Rogan asks, how do women feel about being in combat with men who are not adequate to back *them* up?

[A 1995] Army study indicates that women can develop adequate strength if trained correctly.

[Army researcher] J. Michael Brower says, "One of the oldest myths surrounding the question of women in the military has been that females simply lack, in general, the physical stamina to sustain the most demanding tasks, including combat." Army researchers have destroyed the myth with a new study that indicates women can develop adequate strength if trained correctly. In May 1995, the training began, ninety minutes a day, five days a week. More than 75 percent of the 41 women studied were found fit for traditional male military duties. Before the training 25 percent of the women could perform the tasks. The women ran a two-mile wooded course wearing a 75-pound rucksack and performed squats holding a 100-pound barbell on their shoulders. Women are not allowed, however, to compete for many jobs involving heavy lifting, says Brower. This study along with one carried out by the Ministry of Defence in Great Britain with similar findings should help dispel the myth of women's physical incapacity. Brower reminds us that "without the proper credentials, military women can never be full partners with their male counterparts." Only a small percentage, he continues, of people assigned to combat actually are ever exposed to direct enemy fire, but combat is a necessary assignment for military men and women whose goals are the top military positions. Twenty-five percent of all recruits are female, adds Brower, but without a combat assignment, top key positions will not be available to them.

Brower says that the military's "separate but unequal policy, like the proverbial house divided against itself, cannot long stand the batterings of social progress at work on its bigoted superstructure." The military's most prestigious and meaningful positions are within the combat arms. These positions, says Brower, are not available to women because their job tracks remain restrictive. "High rank may be conceded, but it is the *position* that females are permitted to retain that truly measures their progress within what is still popularly perceived to be a males' game, despite the presence of more women under arms than ever." Many of the arguments against assigning women to combat positions, according to Brower, are a smokescreen, reflect a double standard, and "are as flat as decanted champagne today."

Women who . . . were eager to be assigned to combat units were the most concerned that [physical] standards not be lowered.

Rear Marine Corporal Roxine C. Hart [author of *Women in Combat*] notes that the biological issues, especially strength and endurance, are among the debatable questions concerning women in combat. The usual arguments concerning women's biological capability involve their potential to perform physically and that is affected by prior athletic activity. If women continue to increase their participation in athletics, then they will be more capable. Second, the real issue is how strong does a woman have to be? If we acknowledge that not all men are physically capable for some combat assignments, we should also acknowledge that some women are physically capable. In contrast, opponents say that body composition, size, mass, fat distribution, and structure contribute more to strength, explosive power, speed, throwing and jumping abilities. Cardiorespiratory differences also favor men in size of heart, lungs, oxygen content and uptake, hemoglobin content, body temperature, and sweat gland functions. . . .

Gender and age norming vs. job requirements

In interview after interview, military people told me that the basic consideration in dealing with ability, whether we are evaluating a woman or a man, is the use of gender and age norming. "Gender and age norming are important to ensure the overall fitness (wellness) of service members," according to Major Mary Finch. Finch explains that "all service members in a particular specialty should have to pass the same physical tests, so long as the tests are based on skill and real strength *requirements* for the job, not on old tests that were designed to challenge men and which are not relevant to required strength." The intent of the Army physical fitness test is not to determine qualification for combat.

Finch was asked how would she respond to the statements "Women have an inherent disadvantage because gender norming avoids the real problem (that is, the disadvantage)" and "Since the disadvantage is inherent, women can never be equal to men in the military; therefore we are putting lives in danger, the women's lives and the males who serve with her." She replied: "What is required for the job? Make all soldiers meet those requirements—disadvantage or not. Just make sure there is an honest broker checking that the strength/endurance requirements are based on real requirements for combat."

Proper training enabled women to perform sit-ups to male standards and to improve on other performance.

Brigadier General Wilma L. Vaught, gets to the heart of the issue: "We shouldn't have women or men in a situation where they are not trained or capable of doing the job. So if we are not physically strong enough to do the full scope of the jobs in the infantry, then we shouldn't be there." Further, Vaught believes that ability should be assessed by what someone can do for a thirty-day period, not just a one-day period. "Physical strength and stamina over a sustained period of time [are the criteria], for example, 40-pound shells. I can do it three hours, but can I do it all the time in defense? If a person can't, he or she shouldn't be assigned to that job specialty." She also contends we should ask the question, "Should the job be done that way?" In the late 1970s, she says, "It was felt that women shouldn't lift X amount. As a matter of fact, men couldn't lift certain amounts either. They would get a friend. Men developed low back problems. So we have to ask, "Is the job being done right in the first place?" And "Are the standards what they should be."

Because women are entering additional nontraditional specialties, particularly combat-related ones, President George H.W. Bush's 1993 Presidential Commission on the Assignment of Women in the Armed Forces concluded physical tests should be established for all service members because women tend to have less upper body strength and cardiorespiratory endurance than men. Finch explains that if the Army decided to create specific tests for nontraditional specialties and combat assignments (there are presently no such tests or qualifications), these tests should not be gender or age normed, but should be based on the job requirements. Finch points to the experience of Pfluke, who testified to the Commission that she would accept a transfer to the infantry tomorrow, "only nine weeks after delivering her second son." Finch concludes that she is not sure whether the small numbers of women who would be interested and qualified to join the infantry women would be worth its opening up to them. She reports unanimous agreement, however, that women in combat assignments should meet the same requirements as men. Women who testified and were eager to be assigned to combat units were the most concerned that standards not be lowered.

Brigadier General Mike Hall testified before the Presidential Commission about his experience in 1990, when he was assigned to the Central Command as the theater air liaison officer in Operation Desert Storm [U.S. war to expel Iraq from neighboring Kuwait]. During that time he saw men and women sharing the common bond of living in deprived conditions on a daily basis in order to do something worthwhile for their nation. Hall believes that if women are allowed in direct combat-related assignments, they would perform the air liaison role with ground forces well. Captain Jackie Parker, the first woman to graduate from Test Pilot School, flew the F-16 in school, but after she graduated, she was restricted by assignment to heavy aircraft. Hall testified that Parker was a fully capable pilot. Parker went to Test Pilot School, something Hall did not have the opportunity to do. She had achieved more by age 31 than he had by that age, but he had more opportunities ahead than she. Poignantly, he testified, "And all that opportunity was there for me, it's not there for her, and the difference is I've got the Y chromosome."

Hall testified that the Army physical test (PT) is slightly more sophisticated than the Air Force PT in that it requires sit-ups and push-ups in addition to a timed run. In the fighter business, he says, they have built an aircraft that makes us capable of approaching human limits and can specifically measure qualification for G-tolerance in the centrifuge. There is a significant difference in individual tolerance, but Hall does not believe there is any gender basis for discrimination. "The real issue is whether you, as an individual can pass that test."

Overcoming barriers through training and technology

Is the gender thing a red herring? Major Pfluke says that it is. We don't call age norming a double standard. Differences in physical ability exist between the genders, but some of those same differences exist within each gender. The differences within one gender are the crux of the issue. Interviewees never denied that males help their friends who may be a little less physically able. Add to this fact that there are women who are more able than many men or other women and the issue of women in combat becomes heated rather quickly. Some military interviewees believed that addressing gender issues would prevent me from getting to the real issue, that a female in the military is a soldier first. "The concept of a woman soldier will get lost," one military woman said.

The assignment of a soldier to any position within the military should depend upon his or her [physical and mental] qualifications.

A 1993 USMC study found that proper training enabled women to perform sit-ups to male standards and to improve on other performance. Lieutenant Coronel Greg Morin, Department Director, Military Police, says that combat is an individual thing for men and women. "We are individuals. Some women and men would fit and others would not. Yes, some could, some couldn't." Morin believes it takes time for change. People who do accept women in combat will be in the higher ranks in the future. "The Marine Corps," he notes, "has overcome some major challenges. I think we can overcome that. The military is moving in the direction of women integrating."

Morin also says, "the rapid progression of technology has detracted from the 80-pound pack and 8-mile [test] as a prerequisite for combat. Technology has made it possible for women to fight a battle as well as men. Light vehicles that can move and maneuver make it less necessary for the hike and walk. It is becoming easier," he concluded, "for a woman to be in combat."

In April 1997, the Marines were leading the challenge with their very own pioneering moment. Another barrier limiting the role of women in the military fell. "Enlisted women for the first time shot live ammunition from heavy weapons in the Marine combat training that follows boot camp," says Michael Janofsky. "One of the women, Private Cynthia Martinez, 20, and other women like her reflect the scale of change in the centuries-old military assumption that women could not be warriors." In 1995, Gen Charles Krulak, Commandant of the Marine Corps, overhauled Marine training. Training with 305 men and a "gender-integrated chain-of-command," 54 women were among the first to endure the grueling "Crucible" [final endurance test] combat training after boot camp. The other services conduct mixed-gender recruit training, but Krulak ordered men and women to learn combat skills together. Krulak says Marine recruit training will remain separate.

Admiral Arthur believes the military will never return to zero:

> Women will reach top ranks easier than their male counterparts. With all that has been developed, this [progress] has to move forward so a talented female will be moved forward. But if put in measuring units, for example, race,—how much of the female population will be in control of arms. It will never reach parity. Maybe 50 years from now with a new generation raised in a unisex way [it's possible]. But the way we raise our kids and grandkids today, women will not go to the fox holes. Women will gravitate to what they do best. A few will [go to fox holes] but [numbers of women doing that] will not grow significantly.

Arthur thinks it isn't within our cultural beliefs to assign women in direct combat.

Progress is taking place. The early nineties saw the ban lifted on the assignment of women in some combat positions. Policy is modifying, and a beginning is taking place. To the women working for the cause, more change will come, but slowly. At any rate, the assignment of a soldier to any position within the military should depend upon his or her qualifications, physical ability, and mental and psychological wherewithal for the position. These criteria will give our forces the best state of readiness and our nation the best defense.

3

Women Can Be Integrated into Ground Combat Units

Adam N. Wojack

Adam N. Wojack is a captain in the U.S. Army stationed in Schwein-furt, Germany. He served with the 101st Airborne Division during the 1991 Persian Gulf War.

Opponents of integrating women into ground combat units contend that women lack the upper body strength to perform an infantryman's job, that they are too valuable as reproducers of human life, and that they will destroy the cohesion of all-male ground combat units. On closer examination, these contentions rest on false assumptions. If the army instituted a women-only training program before the start of integrated training, women would significantly close the physical performance gap with men. Secondly, since the actual percentage of women in direct combat would be quite low, the threat to women's traditional roles as procreators would be negligible. Finally, as long as women are treated fairly and equally and men do not perceive them as receiving special treatment, there is no reason why men and women cannot bond to form effective combat units.

This viewpoint proposes that the U.S. Army integrate women into the infantry branch. It will dispel practical notions that a woman is too "weak" to do an infantryman's job and that her presence will destroy team spirit and ground maneuver units' fighting effectiveness. This viewpoint does not dispute those who believe it is wrong for the United States to send women to fight close combat battles, nor is it an advocate for those who wish to destroy gender barriers simply because they exist. It acknowledges the personal nature of those points of view and avoids them altogether. Instead, this viewpoint assumes a sociopolitical climate in which only practical debate is waged about whether to integrate women into the infantry. The issue, then, is not about right and wrong but about suitability and feasibility. Can women do the infantryman's job, and how can the Army help them do it? The key assumption, here, is that American women would volunteer to become infantry soldiers if given the chance.

Why women in the infantry?

Ground combat units contain the only jobs closed to women in land-based military forces today. Before the All-Volunteer Force (AVF) [instituted in 1973] which recruited women to replace some of the Army's postdraft manpower losses, women made up 3 percent of all soldiers in the Army. Today, women account for 14 percent of all soldiers and 20 percent of all recruits. They fly attack helicopters, command military police companies, drive infantry soldiers into combat on trucks, and "man" logistics bases far forward, or in the midst, of ground maneuver forces. In the past 15 years, women have been killed in combat. At the end of Operation Desert Storm in 1991 [U.S. military action to expel Iraq from neighboring Kuwait], there were 13 women killed in action. Of those, four were termed "hostile deaths" out of a total of 148 U.S. combat deaths. Interestingly, two of those deaths occurred when an Iraqi Scud missile hit a temporary barracks housing combat service support units far behind the forward edge of the battle area.

Women are in close proximity to combat regardless of where they are on the battlefield, so they might as well be allowed to fight offensively.

These deaths seem to back the notion that today's battlefield is no longer as well-defined as it once was. For example, U.S. offensive doctrine calls for attacking the enemy's lines of communication, in addition to his main defenses, to disrupt their combat forces' resupply. The theory is that, if successful, the enemy's maneuver forces will run out of rations, ammunition, and the will to fight, in that order. It is no secret that the United States' conventional threat uses the same doctrine. Our field trains, brigade support areas, and division support areas are the key objectives of conventional enemy attacks. It is also no secret that most Army women work in these areas.

This doctrine transforms all soldiers—men and women—in field command and control and/or logistics areas into front-line combatants, at least in the enemy's eyes. Why attack through infantry and armor when the division rear can be penetrated? Of course, this says nothing about why women belong in the infantry.

Proponents of giving women the right to serve in ground combat units usually use a combination of arguments: an equal opportunity to serve is every American's right; current technologies are gender-neutral; and other nations allow women in the infantry. This list omits perhaps the most compelling reason to integrate women into the infantry and other ground combat fields: given the contemporary operating environment, women are in close proximity to combat regardless of where they are on the battlefield, so they might as well be allowed to fight offensively.

At this point, opponents of gender integration point out why women do not belong in the infantry:
 • Women lack the upper body strength to perform an infantryman's job.

- Women have certain hygiene needs that would demand special treatment in the field.
- Women are too valuable as reproducers of human life to be wasted in ground combat.
- Women are nondeployable while pregnant.
- Women would destroy the cohesion of previously all-male ground combat units.

The oldest argument against allowing women in the infantry is that women are too weak. The genesis of this argument is as old as society and civilization—women are the weaker sex; a woman's duty is to bear and raise children; men are supposed to protect women. Whether these assumptions are myth or reality, they have governed social thought for centuries. Women did not serve in the military, and women did not play sports. Women who chose to work were restricted to teaching, clerking, and nursing. Even when women were allowed in the military during World War II, they did not receive the same military training as the men. Instead, women received pointers on how to maintain trim figures and an attractive appearance.

Women were partly responsible for this. In World War II, the Navy's Women Accepted for Voluntary Emergency Service (WAVES) initially attracted more women than the Army's Women's Army Corps (WAC). The WAVES' navy blue uniform was considered more stylish than the olive drab the WACs wore.

The women's movement of the late 1960s and early 1970s changed all of that. American women demanded equal treatment and equal opportunity in all aspects of society and very nearly got that. In 1972, Congress enacted a law known as Title IX that made it illegal for any school that received Federal funds to spend more money on men's athletics than it did on women's athletics. More than anything before or since, Title IX made it acceptable and attractive for women to pursue athletic dreams and hone their athletic prowess at the high school and collegiate levels. In the 25-plus years since Title IX was introduced, women's athletics in America have grown exponentially. Today, women in high school and college compete in many of the same sports in which men compete, and women now play professional soccer and basketball in national, televised leagues.

Since [1972 and the congressional law known as] Title IX, women have been able to realize their physiological potential in athletics.

Title IX's key contribution was giving women the government's stamp of approval to be athletic without risking losing their "womanness." Meanwhile, women gained much athletic ground on men. Consider the world record progression in the marathon. In the past 30 years, the men's record has gone from 2 hours, 9 minutes (2:09) to 2:05, a 3-percent improvement. Over the same period, the women's record has improved from 3:01 to 2:18, an almost 24-percent improvement. The women's record went from being 71 percent of the men's record to 90 percent.

Note also the pole vault event, which was closed to women because track and field authorities considered women either to be too weak or the event too dangerous, or both. Since the International Association of Athletics Federations opened the event to women in 1992, the women's record has gone from an initial 4.05 meters (m) to 4.81 m, a 16-percent improvement. In the same period, the men's record improved only .04 percent, from 6.12 m to 6.14 m.

This is not to say that women will continue to improve at the pace of the past 30 years and bypass men's athletic accomplishments. What this shows is a true picture of women's athletic potential. Simply put, before Title IX, women were not encouraged to play and, on the whole, played at a misleadingly low level compared to men. Since Title IX, women have been able to realize their physiological potential in athletics.

The Army has no one to blame but itself for any shortcomings in the perceived or tested physical abilities of female soldiers.

Sports scientists generally agree that a woman can run 90 percent as fast as a man over all distances and is about two-thirds as strong in the upper body. However, upper body strength assessments might soon prove to be inaccurate. Women's weightlifting world records hover at around 70 percent of the men's record in most comparable weight classes. In some classes, the women's record is as high as 78 percent. Bear in mind that weightlifting, like pole vaulting, was introduced to the Olympic Games as a medal sport for women only during 2000.

Scientists point out that a woman's athletic potential is limited by specific physiology. American women are, on average, 4 inches shorter than the average man and 40 pounds lighter. Women also have from 6.5 to 13 pounds more body fat than men and from 40 to 48 pounds less lean body mass, or muscle weight. Women also possess about one-tenth of the amount of testosterone as men, a hormone that is key to strength development. Because of this, scientists say that even the strongest, fastest woman can never expect to surpass the strongest, fastest man.

However, even if physiology allows a woman to be two-thirds as strong as an average man, most women are actually much less strong than that. Sports physiologists believe this condition is culturally induced. In our society, strength is viewed as a masculine trait, and small, frail bodies are considered to be feminine. Sex stereotypes such as these do much to program behavior and prevent individuals from fulfilling their full potential. In the past, this has meant discouraging women from engaging in weight training and the more strenuous sports (football, basketball, soccer) that men have traditionally played. While there has been progress since Title IX, change is slow.

Change is even slower in the Army. The AVF and Title IX occurred at around the same time. Both acknowledged a need for greater and more varied roles for women in society and in the Armed Forces. While Title IX spawned a generation of professional women athletes, the AVF seemed content to protect the status quo. Consider the Army Physical Fitness Test (APFT). The current APFT, introduced in 1999, is only a revision of the

1984 paradigm that introduced 2 minutes each of pushups and situps and the timed 2-mile run.

The Army developed the 1984 standards by testing a large group of soldiers without familiarizing or training them on the new events and then recording the scores. The Army APFT minimum standard became the number of pushups and situps and 2-mile run time recorded by soldiers at the bottom of the 90 percent that passed. In sum, the Army's landmark 1984 APFT makeover, intended to bring soldiers to a higher level of health and physical readiness, was based on the achievements of the 11th percentile.

Men's standards were actually high enough to be both challenging and realistic. The youngest men, 18 to 21 years old, had to perform a minimum of 42 pushups and 52 situps, and run 2 miles in 15:54 to pass the APFT. However, women's standards were much lower. The youngest women had to do 18 pushups and 50 situps and run 2 miles in 18:54.

Comparatively, women did 43 percent of the upper body work the men did, performed roughly the same amount of abdominal work, and ran 84 percent of the men's minimum. These scores do not correspond with a woman's physiological potential. Assuming that most soldiers train to meet rather than exceed APFT standards, Army women since 1984 have done only about 64 percent of the upper body work of which they are capable and about 90 percent of their ability on the 2-mile run.

By the mid-1990s, the Army, realizing its standards were too low in some places and too high in others, rewrote the APFT's minimum standards. As of 1999, women and men were required to do the same number of situps across all age groups. The Army also increased the minimum number of pushups for the youngest women—by one. The 2-mile run time minimums remained the same. In determining the new standards, the Army used the 1984 testing strategy, eliminating the bottom 10 percent as failures and adopting the next lowest score as the minimum standard. Participants were not put through a special physical training program to raise standards. Soldiers had performed against the 1984 standards throughout their periods of service and performed predictably.

Given this study, one could say the Army has no one to blame but itself for any shortcomings in the perceived or tested physical abilities of female soldiers. In short, the Army has not given women a chance to succeed physically on a par with men.

Physique, which is only one argument against introducing women into the infantry, is also the one the critics are most ready to concede in light of the great strides women have made in athletics in the past 30 years. Other issues—nondeployability, special hygiene and privacy needs, and their status as procreators—also deserve attention.

Pregnancy, privacy, and hygiene issues

Opponents of women in the infantry cite nondeployability because of pregnancy as a reason not to have female grunts, but consider the 1991 Persian Gulf war. Overall deployability rates throughout the Gulf war were 91 percent for women and 98 percent for men. Reportedly, half of all soldiers who did not deploy had medical problems. Because of the 7-percent disparity, the consensus among men—without proof—was that many women were getting pregnant so they would not have to deploy. It is likely that some women did just that. Even so, the pregnancy rate for women in the military during the Gulf war remained the same as the peacetime rate. It has even been suggested that, as a temporary disability, men missed more work time due to sports injuries than women missed while pregnant.

Well-trained women could become America's greatest source of asymmetric [unconventional] combat power [in the fight against terrorists].

Privacy and hygiene needs are the next issue. In short, men and women require separate latrines, showers, and living quarters, especially in the field. This was also tested during the Gulf war. The Army discovered that by using common sense and having respect for each others' needs, men and women soldiers could share limited field latrines and showers without incident. Billeting is a concern only when it is limited to tents or actual field conditions. Commanders in the Gulf tried several different strategies: separate tents when available; women's sections of tents separated by hanging towels or blankets and integrated tents where privacy was minimal.

In the end, women found they preferred sharing tents with those they worked with and handling any privacy issues in the same common-sense manner as was used with latrines and showers. Rumors of sexual liaisons in tent cities were common during the Gulf war, but two reasons probably kept such behavior to a minimum: the lack of privacy and familiarity within any unit. In the words of one woman assigned to a unit deployed to the Gulf, "We know their wives and girlfriends so we don't expect trouble."

The third issue is women's place as procreators and nurturers. Opponents say women are too valuable to society to risk in direct combat because they bear children. But this issue pulls at emotions rather than at intellect. In the early 1990s, Air Force Chief of Staff General Merrill A. Mc-Peak spoke for many when he said, "I just can't get over this feeling of old men ordering young women into combat. . . . I have a gut-based hangup there. And it doesn't make a lot of sense in every way. I apologize for it." In its original manifestation, the Equal Rights Amendment narrowly missed being approved, perhaps because of this one issue. But the issue is very much alive.

The actual percentage of women in direct combat would probably be quite low. No one can imagine the total number of women in ground combat units surpassing 25 percent of all personnel anytime in the distant future after any type of integration. With 10 divisions in the Active Army totaling 500,000, 25 percent equates to 20,000 women in direct combat roles. Twenty thousand women represents about .03 percent of the approximately 60 million American women who are currently in their reproductive prime. Of course, a world war would more than likely pull more women into ground combat units, but in that case, global and human survival would be at stake. In comparison to peacetime, the number of women who would voluntarily serve in ground combat units is low. For example, Canada, a nation with an armed force of about 65,000, currently has six women infantry soldiers.

On the flip side of this issue, women are the most valuable human military asset because some of the gravest threats today come not from conventional armies but from asymmetric forces such as global terrorists. This type of threat uses surprise to achieve its goals. The current threat also operates from Third-World, religiously fundamental countries or societies where women's rights do not exist. Such male-dominated, paternalistic, and sexist threat groups probably do not expect to meet resistance from women, especially those who are not dressed in traditional military garb. Well-trained women could become America's greatest source of asymmetric combat power.

Racial integration as example

The last issue that opponents of gender integration bring up is cohesion. They wonder if allowing women into ground combat roles improves or undermines combat readiness. The hard truth is that right now, integrating women into the infantry and other currently all-men combat arms units would more than likely hurt morale initially. Infantrymen and leaders would fumble their way to finding out just how to deal with women. The news media would pay close attention and generate excessive publicity, both positive and negative. It would be a bumpy ride for a while, but more than likely, the Army and the infantry would adjust. The U.S. Army would be better for it, not worse.

The obvious comparison to total gender integration is the Armed Forces' racial integration that President Harry S. Truman ordered in 1948. Based on unit cohesion alone this was a risky move that most whites and many blacks opposed. Whites argued that black soldiers were unreliable and careless, and blacks maintained they would not get fair treatment in racially integrated units. After integration, blacks and whites agreed that black soldiers performed better in racially mixed units because competition with white soldiers improved not only their soldier skills but their self-confidence as well.

Women and men can bond to form effective [military] units . . . as long as the women feel they will be treated equally.

Researchers at the time also found that desegregation did not hurt combat effectiveness. Residual racism still existed, but it was offset by the realization that blacks could be as competent at soldiering as whites and that formal integration was improving black soldiers' skills. Interestingly, black soldiers' complaints of racism or unfair treatment actually decreased in integrated units.

Following this example, gender integration could be as simple and successful as racial integration. But women are not separated from men by skin color alone. In gender integration, women actually have less in common with men than white and black men did with each other in 1948. White and black men were already infantry soldiers. Women, if they are to be accepted by men in previously all-male fields, must not only prove themselves equal to men, they must also demolish generations-old perceptions of being the protected rather than the protector. This is the recipe for cohesion.

Effects on cohesion

Social scientists today prefer to divide cohesion, or the feelings that bind individuals to the immediate group, into two types: task and social. Opponents argue that introducing women into ground combat units would immediately erode those units' social cohesion, which they argue is more important than task cohesion. Opponents also say that any well-trained group of men and women can develop task cohesion to accomplish virtually any work problem, regardless of how members feel about each other. They go on to say that while task cohesion may be enough to get the job done in the civilian work force, it is not enough in the military. In the military, the intimacy and isolation of combat demand high social cohesion. This leaves only one question: Can women bond socially with men?

According to a 1997 (RAND) study that the Department of Defense sponsored, "Gender differences alone did not appear to erode cohesion. Cohesion was reported high in units where people believed the command emphasized unity and the importance and necessity of all members and divisions in accomplishing the mission." Even more important, the study went on to say, "High social cohesion, or bonding on a social level, can have deleterious effects on performance outcomes and task cohesion, because people start to prioritize friendship and social activities over performing their jobs."

Integrating women into [the U.S. Army's] infantry need not be difficult or painful as long as it is approached with common sense.

The bottom line regarding either social or task cohesion is fair and equal treatment. Women and men can bond to form effective units in any job field or situation as long as the women feel they will be treated equally and the men perceive that the women will not receive special treatment.

There is one additional lesson about gender integration and unit cohesion that our service academies and military colleges have taught us. Once women comprise more than 20 percent of a unit or class, they are judged as individuals and not as representatives of their gender. Successful women cadets in the group become fellow cadets, not female cadets. Overall unit acceptance soon follows.

On the matter of cohesion, caution goes with promise. The lessons that service academies and NATO allies have learned, particularly in Canada, as they went through gender-integration trials, tells us that it takes roughly a year to break down preexisting, negative, sexist attitudes.

It takes quite a while before mixed-gender units function more efficiently and at higher levels of capability than all-male units. Therefore, says one social scientist, "Until American women are given the opportunity to dispel the prejudicial opinions ensconced within the U.S. military, those opposed to extended integration assist in the perpetuation of these preconceived notions."

Integrating women into the infantry: Canada's example

Contrary to what many believe, only Canada has succeeded at desegregating its infantry. When the topic of military fighting women comes up, many point to Israel as an example of a nation with a gender-integrated ground combat force. But this is not true. Israeli women have not served in combat roles since Israel's War of Independence in 1948, and even then, most say they served because of desperate need. Today, unmarried Israeli women are drafted and serve short tours in the Israel Defense Forces, but they are restricted to clerical and noncombat medical fields. They are excluded from any duty involving imminent danger. In reality, American women have far greater military opportunities than do Israeli women.

Canada, the only modern nation with women in its infantry ranks, began its gender-assimilation program in 1989 and met mostly with failure. It eventually succeeded on a small scale, learning hard lessons along the way. These lessons are the key to successful gender integration in other armies.

First, Canada's volunteer women went through regular segregated basic training, performing no more than minimum women's standards before integrated infantry training. Women's physical fitness standards in Canada are lower than men's, so the women arrived at infantry school already behind the men in overall fitness.

Once in the integrated infantry school, the women were piecemealed among the training platoons. The average composition of a platoon contained only two or three women to 30 to 40 men. This led the women to feel little or no peer support.

Finally, the Canadian forces selected too many women who could not meet the physical standards needed to perform an infantryman's job. This was probably because of a lack of volunteers. Some Canadian women dropped out of the program early, feeling that videos of infantry training and recruiters' descriptions misled them.

Also, sexual harassment in Canada's infantry was a problem that was not addressed. The first woman to become an officer in Canada's infantry was a young woman named Sandra Perron. For years, coworkers subjected Perron to what she termed "constant emotional and psychological harassment." Perron did not complain; instead, she quit the army in 1995. Several years later she spoke out about the abuse. She recounted one incident of being tied to a tree, beaten, and left in the snow without boots for 4 hours. An investigation revealed that peers who were competing with her for promotions resented Perron.

Canada reacted to the Perron incident by instituting policies and training designed to eliminate sexual harassment. Current women infantry soldiers in Canada credit Perron for breaking down barriers and forcing the army to rethink its position on sexual harassment. Still others feel Perron handled the situation incorrectly. Another woman infantry officer, Maureen Wellwood, told a reporter, "The key is to talk about it. Sandra Perron should not have kept quiet. . . . She was very strong, but she accepted it at the beginning, and it kept going." Wellwood said that there are still many men who oppose women in the infantry. "And there still will be years from now. But now the people who harass get into trouble, and not the other way around."

Of interest is the still minuscule total number of women serving in Canada's infantry: six. In an armed force of 65,000, that number achieves the critical mass of 20 percent in only one echelon: a single platoon. It appears that Canada's infantry women will be isolated for some time. Even so, the Canadian Government has taken notice and is learning. In a 1999 article on recruiting women into its armed forces, the Canadian Department of National Defence was quoted as "hoping 25 percent of all new enlistees will be women."

The U.S. Army can benefit from Canada's experience. In fact, integrating women into its infantry need not be difficult or painful as long as it is approached with common sense and a common purpose. That common purpose should be success. It should not integrate women into traditionally all-male units unless it is serious about creating an environment for their success. It can accomplish this by synthesizing the arguments and lessons learned.

The plan

Adopt higher APFT standards for women. Use the current 1999 standards for men as a starting point, and set the women's minimum standard for the run at 90 percent of the men's—17:40 rather than 18:54. Make the pushup standard for women 70 percent of the men's standard—29 rather than 19. Situp standards should remain equal. These standards are overall improvements that the Army needs to increase women's physical condition. This will give the Army a more physically fit force and dispel the notion that women soldiers have a lower, easier standard than men.

Infantry one-station unit training (OSUT) for enlisted women should be preceded by a women-only physical fitness trainup of from 4 to 8 weeks. This would close the physical readiness gap between men and women before integrated training starts. Women would be indoctrinated into the infantry physical workload by training against men's APFT standards with weight training and rucksack marching. Only those women who meet the minimum standards of the men's APFT would graduate. From there, graduates would be integrated into infantry OSUT at Fort Benning, Georgia, along with the men trainees. Many women could start OSUT in better physical shape than the male trainees. This should improve initial unit cohesion by inspiring competition and respect among the untrained men and the physically ready women.

No fewer than eight women trainees, or a sufficient number to reach 20 percent of the whole, would be assigned to any training platoon—approximately 40 soldiers—at OSUT. This is consistent with social scientists' critical mass observation on the number of minorities in a majority group that are necessary to ensure adequate peer support for the minority and acceptance by the majority.

Women in OSUT would receive the same haircuts as the men, would not be allowed to wear makeup, and would compete against the same physical standards as the men. This uses lessons learned from successful gender integration at the Virginia Military Institute (VMI) in the mid-1990s. VMI benefited from the hard lessons The Citadel [military college] learned after its much-publicized forced integration of Shannon Faulkner in 1995. VMI treated the women like the men but monitored harassment. VMI leaders discovered that the men immediately accepted women who succeeded under those conditions.

Once women reach critical mass . . . in the overall infantry, unit cohesion and combat readiness should improve in ways we probably cannot imagine.

Cadre at OSUT would include women drill sergeants and officers who had successfully completed infantry OSUT or the officer equivalent. Each training company with women basic trainees would have at least one woman drill sergeant and one officer. The initial low numbers of women in OSUT could result in concentrating all women trainees into one training company. That would not be counterproductive. In fact, it might foster peer support and the majority's peer approval.

Women in OSUT would train to achieve the men's standards throughout training but would meet the women's standards in their age groups to pass the final APFT. Women would meet all other standards required of men, including the 5-mile run in 45 minutes and all road marches carrying the same equipment as the men.

Upon graduation, women infantry soldiers would be grouped into cohorts and assigned to the same field unit. The 20-percent guideline would be strictly adhered to. If a battalion received a cohort of six women, all would be assigned to one company and one platoon. This 20 percent guideline would be an integration tool rather than a permanent procedure. Once women were successfully integrated into the infantry, they would be individually assigned and reassigned just as other soldiers are.

Women infantry officer trainees would precede women enlisted infantry trainees. Women at the U.S. Military Academy; in the Reserve Officer Training Course; and in Officer Candidate School would be allowed to enter the infantry branch. Upon commissioning, women officers would attend the Infantry Officer Basic Course (IOBC) at Fort Benning. They would continue to be assigned using the 20-percent guideline. Women IOBC graduates would then go to Ranger School, using the principles described. For all female infantry officer training, women cadre members would be essential, especially at Ranger School. Successfully integrating women officers into infantry units would establish a path for young women to follow and ensure commissioned officer support.

Finally, each unit containing women infantry soldiers would designate a field grade officer within that unit to issue integration instruction and to oversee gender integration. The field grade officer would also coach, teach, and mentor women infantry soldiers and their leaders throughout the process. Company commanders would be directly responsible for their women infantry soldiers' training and welfare.

If integrating women into the infantry proceeded as outlined, not only would women succeed, but sexual harassment in the Army would decline. The greater respect women earn for themselves as true equals with military men will foster this.

The infantry will most likely struggle at first, but once women reach critical mass in units and in the overall infantry, unit cohesion and combat readiness should improve in ways we now probably cannot imagine. Change is part and parcel of the U.S. Army. Just as racial integration in the Armed Forces was considered dangerous 50 years ago, integrating females into ground combat units seems crazy today. For sure, the debate will continue, and opponents will continue to fight it. However, they are running out of solid arguments as well as time.

4

Women Will Reduce the Effectiveness of Ground Combat Units

Anna Simons

Anna Simons is an associate professor in the Special Operations Academic Group at the Naval Postgraduate School in Monterey, California. She is the author of The Company They Keep: Life Inside the U.S. Army Special Forces.

Significant problems will arise for the military if women are integrated into ground combat units. Because pregnancy will render a woman nondeployable, it will be difficult to convince men that a woman's gender will not excuse her from duty at some point and disrupt the readiness of combat units. Privacy will also become an issue, since given close quarters and shared showers, men and women will be constantly reminded of one another's sex. This unavoidable intimacy will have a detrimental effect on the cohesion and togetherness necessary for effective combat units. Men will find themselves competing against one another for the attentions of women, raising the potential for jealousy, rearranging loyalties, and reducing all-important group trust.

Among the easiest predictions to make in this first year of the new century is that various interest groups will continue to lobby to open all US combat units to women. At least five seemingly logical arguments can be anticipated:
- New post–Cold War missions require finesse, not brawn.
- Twenty-first-century technologies are gender-neutral.
- An equal opportunity to serve is every American citizen's right.
- Cohesion does not require that soldiers bond socially, only that they accomplish their tasks effectively.
- Our European allies are opening their combat units to women, therefore so should we.

Anna Simons, "Women in Combat Units: It's Still a Bad Idea," *Parameters*, vol. 31, no. 2, Summer 2001, pp. 89–100. Copyright © 2001 by U.S. Army War College. Reproduced by permission of the author.

Targeting combat exclusion laws

Each of these arguments flies in the face of common sense, however, and together they beg the central question, which is how would the integration of women improve a combat unit's survivability and the defense of the United States.

For instance, if war in the future will be push-button and relatively effortless, then why have combat units at all? Why not just disband them altogether or, at the very least, phase them out? Likewise, if our soldiers' primary duty will be to keep peace and thus avoid war, then why not train them in nothing but non-lethal techniques?

Tellingly, not even those who envision a radically altered high-tech battlescape advocate the dissolution of combat units. None among them has called for an end to teaching hand-to-hand combat, movement-to-contact, or night patrolling skills. None is really arguing that we won't need some sort of close-in as well as sustained combat capability. Rather, the push now is to integrate capable women into such units. Why?

There are at least two sets of answers. The first has to do with knocking down the walls of one of the last all-male preserves. For those opposed on principle to men's exclusivity, as well as their presumed dominance, the only important war to be waged is the gender war, and what could be a more appropriate target than the combat exclusion laws? Those who argue this point of view are relatively easy to dismiss, since they are uninterested in engaging in discussions about the role of the military.

Those who want to see women serve in combat units [fail to] explain the price they believe combat units pay for women's current absence.

Impossible to ignore, on the other hand, are those who are passionate about the military either because they serve or feel every American should have the opportunity to do so. From their perspective, fairness dictates that American women be granted the same opportunities to fulfill their citizenship duties—and in the same ways—as American men.

But if this is their position, why shouldn't everyone have to fulfill these duties? Why aren't they advocating national service or universal conscription? If either were in place, their logic would be unassailable and not just persuasive. If all Americans were required to serve, women could legally demand equivalent opportunities, and it is hard to imagine their being denied. However, with the force structured as it is, everyone doesn't have to volunteer, all volunteers don't have to be accepted, and women know from the outset they will not be allowed into certain units.

On closer examination, it seems that the struggle is less about rights and responsibilities than it is about rewards. Women in uniform, and female officers especially, are understandably concerned about promotion and advancement. Nor are equity and justice unreasonable goals or career demands. In fact, they are eminently reasonable. But the push being made to enable women to serve with men in combat units belies the stated desire, which is for women to attain the same opportunities as men. If the aim was truly parity and opportunity, women could accomplish both equally well in their own single-gender combat units. Yet, the notion of developing such units is never broached in this country, which is itself suggestive. The real intent must therefore be to earn women the chance to compete directly against men for a shot at positions of higher command. Otherwise, why not lobby for all-female units? Being able to live up to one's citizenship duties by "sharing" in combat doesn't require having to fight from the same foxholes—if it did, no one would use the term "The Greatest Generation" to pay homage to [World War II] veterans from Omaha Beach and Guadalcanal, as well as to the nurses who treated their wounds or the women who worked back home in steel mills and airplane factories.

Avoiding the issue of effectiveness

The issue of whether women in combat roles might actually improve combat effectiveness is another topic on which proponents of women in combat remain conspicuously silent. That they avoid this only further clarifies what they really seek: namely, a rise in status which they believe is automatic for those choosing to serve in the combat arms. This isn't what anyone says, of course, though if proponents did they might actually have a point. Historically there has always been some degree of bias accorded men who serve in combat units, and those who have seen combat especially. But to redress this (if it should be redressed, which is a big "if"), would require rethinking the nature of status throughout the armed forces—including among men, not just between men and women. Anything less would hardly be fair. Perhaps this explains why those who would overturn the status quo vis-a-vis women don't pursue status equity further.

By now it should be clear. If those opposed to the combat exclusion laws were to push any of their arguments to its logical conclusion, they would lose gender as a pressure point. Worse, they would be forced to acknowledge they don't have answers to the most pressing questions their cause raises. For instance, on the topic of inequity: anyone who has ever held a job, sat in a classroom, or grown up with siblings knows that morale and performance suffer in the face of favoritism. Just the perception of unfairness is often enough to poison the atmosphere. This is worst when it unfolds right in front of you. In the combat arms this would happen at the team, squad, and platoon level. But do lift-the-ban proponents think about fairness in good-of-the-group terms? Do they base their arguments on what is best for these combat units?

The broader point—that most women wouldn't make it "over the high bar"—still sticks, which then [raises] . . . fears surrounding reduced standards.

Those who want to see women serve in combat units neither explain the price they believe combat units pay for women's current absence, nor tell us what a squad would gain by having females present. The most obvious question they leave hanging is one to which every adult should already intuitively know the answer: What would women contribute to a rifle platoon or a SEAL team? The short answer is: distraction, dissension, and distrust. The longer answer has to do with cohesion, bonding, and the vulnerability of men.

Not surprisingly, this is not quite how the subject area experts who oppose the idea of women in combat usually state their case. If only they were more forthcoming, the debate might already be closed.

Something else which attenuates the debate, meanwhile, is the fact that men and women successfully work together under stress, in tight quarters, or for long periods of time in the corporate world, on construction sites, in operating rooms, and in risky and demanding jobs throughout the military. To those unfamiliar with it, combat may represent just a more intense version of these other occupations. Nothing, of course, could be further from the truth. Combat is not a workplace. None of the routine separations the rest of us can count on—whether between day and night, safety and danger, duty and off-duty, or colleagues and bunkmates—pertains. No other environment is so unforgivingly relentless. Thus, though some might believe arguments offered to keep women out of combat units apply more broadly, they would be wrong. Frontline and behind-the-line units differ in kind, not by degree, from other units. Unfortunately, this distinction, which should not only inform but drive the debate, is often either implied by opponents or ignored by advocates, and is seldom addressed head-on.

Reconsidering differences

When men who are or have been in combat units explain why women shouldn't be interjected into their midst, they invariably take one of three initial tacks. They cite what women allegedly lack—speed, strength, and stamina; what they can have—babies, menstrual periods, and breast milk; or what they presumably need—more showers, different facilities, and privacy.

Even recent Reserve Officer Training Corps (ROTC) cadets who have been raised to view women as peers worry about women being too weak to heft heavy weapons, let alone carry one of them should he be wounded. If pushed, however, they readily admit that each has seen at least one woman who could conceivably outperform male peers physically. Bring up female Olympians and the argument over women's inherent physical inabilities falls apart. Of course, the broader point—that most women wouldn't make it "over the high bar"—still sticks, which then becomes an automatic segue to resentments and fears surrounding reduced standards and the consequences of gender-norming. All of these objections about physical capabilities would be rendered moot, however, if only women were held to the exact same physical standards as men and the standards were made as stringent as they had ever been.

The problems raised by women's reproductive capabilities are somewhat harder to resolve—not because women don't know how to avoid pregnancy or manage menstrual pain, but because the military's method of dealing with women who are pregnant or debilitated sends a series of signals it can't control. For instance, in hard-charging combat units, soldiers and marines will often suffer chronic pain and forgo a visit to the doctor in order to avoid being put on profile. Women can't hide their pregnancy in the same way; they can't "suck it up." Instead, pregnancy requires that they be removed from duty and then granted maternity leave.

Also, pregnancy can hardly be considered a random or accidental event that might happen overnight or in training to any soldier. No comparable "disability" renders men non-deployable. Consequently, it becomes virtually impossible to convince men that a woman's gender won't excuse her from duty at some point. Worse, because this potential can be realized at any time, all women have to be considered potentially non-deployable for some length of time. The problem this poses is that it flies in the face of why members of a unit intensively train together at all, which is so they grow familiar with one another while perfecting tactics, techniques, and procedures.

The military faces a perpetual problem. Does it treat men and women as though they do or don't register one another's sex?

Presumptions about women absenting themselves have similarly haunted the corporate world. Nor does it help that many women extend their maternity leave and then willingly surrender high-status positions (or resign their commissions) after giving birth in order to spend more time at home. Worse than just disrupting the work flow, this bespeaks an ease at shifting allegiances which men may mistakenly read into women who have no intention of becoming mothers. Unfortunately, and when weighed in the balance, individual intent is only just that, whereas the potential for bearing children (contraception or no) is incontrovertible biological fact. Nothing on the Y chromosome affects men the same way.

Privacy issues

Nature thus makes for at least one unbridgeable chasm between the sexes that no amount of legislation can overcome. In contrast, one might think differences which everyone would agree are more cultural than natural would be easier to manage. For instance, American women may have been raised to dislike dirt, but this doesn't mean they need to bathe any more often than men. Therefore, it should be easy to mandate no extra showers, no extra water, no extra time, and no separate facilities.

But does that mean no separation? By rights, if all soldiers are to be treated alike, combat soldiers could easily argue that women deserve no more privacy from them than they have from one another. Since squad members sleep next to each other, why not bathe together, as each gender already does (separately) in open shower areas? If the theorizing done by those who want to see women in the 505th Infantry Regiment, Special Forces, or the Ranger battalions is correct, gender need have no effect on individuals' interactions. With proper training people can be taught to think beyond gender, which is only a cultural construct anyway. Following this skein of logic it shouldn't matter that soldiers in the field tend to sleep clothed whereas they shower naked. Nudity per se shouldn't cause men and women who have been told to regard one another as fellow-

soldiers and fellow-soldiers only to bat an eye, let alone raise an eyebrow—
or to wink.

Without doubt were the military to run a Starship Troopers-like ex-
periment along these lines, those bent on erasing gender differences would
be proved correct. In a communal shower, men and women wouldn't see
gender. Instead, they'd be looking at one another's parts.

---

*[Combat] intimacy can't be a prelude to sex. And it
won't be—as long as heterosexual men are kept
separated from women.*

Even if the current academic distinction holds—that gender refers to
what people make of sexual differences, while sexual differences are bio-
logically based but do not determine behavior—the military faces a perpetual problem. Does it treat men and women as though they do or don't
register one another's sex? Even with BDUs [camouflage fatigues] as camouflage, sexual dimorphism is impossible to hide. In close quarters, faces,
voices, hairstyles, sizes, and shapes are all giveaways and continual re-
minders. Of course, this doesn't mean these differences have to matter.
But it does mean that they can. And with nature abhorring a vacuum, if
they can, they likely, eventually, will. How else explain rules forbidding
dating and fraternization; if the potential didn't exist, why bother?

It is almost as if there is widespread tacit agreement on all sides that
men and women can't quite be trusted together. Accepting this as a
given, some who oppose women in combat argue that it is not just sex
that's bound to rear its ugly head, there's also jealousy to contend with,
which will in turn disrupt cohesion. Most adults can offer ample anecdotal evidence of liaisons occurring in mixed-sex groups—and critics like
pointing to integrated Navy ships in particular. But beyond the anec-
dotes, the degree to which illicit affairs actually disrupt operations on
ships or in the workplace is less than clear. Morale is certainly affected,
but operations continue—which suggests that long-standing assumptions
about the links between morale (or cohesion) and effectiveness be recon-
sidered, or a better case be made that combat units really are different
from any other kind of organization, in or out of the military.

Rethinking cohesion

Academics who study or write about the military often distinguish among
morale (how an individual feels), cohesion (feelings that bind individuals
to the immediate, or primary, group), and esprit de corps (feelings that
bind individuals to the larger unit—e.g., a company or battalion). In the
not-so-distant past it was said cohesion possibly resulted from "proximity
of group members over time; social similarities or commonalities; success
at joint tasks; and concerned, competent, honest leaders." However, academics recently have begun splitting such definitions and differentiating
between two types of cohesion: social and task. One aim in doing this is
to underline the fact that everyone need not like one another or be alike
in order to attain a common goal. A corollary aim is to point out that the

degree of attention traditionally paid to peer bonding is overblown.

Perhaps this is so in the worlds of sports, politics, and business. But despite the usual analogies which are made, nothing in the civilian world replicates the hazards of combat, or its demands. Members of police and fire departments may come close in terms of the risks they run on duty. But "on duty" means they work in shifts. War doesn't occur in shifts. Neither does military training. Law enforcement personnel, even when partners, have the luxury of being able to escape one another for predictable, guaranteed periods of time. They may work excessive hours. But their families know where they are; they even see them on a regular basis. On field training exercises, combat soldiers will be out of touch (never mind sight) from loved ones for days. Deployed, they leave home for months. Worse, they're stuck with only each other for company.

Combat units form singular entities in more ways than can be cataloged, both literally and figuratively. In Special Force (SF), for instance, teams routinely practice going into isolation, though anyone who has spent time in an SF company knows teams happily stick to their team rooms; there are no common areas. But even figuratively, combat units exhibit intense clannishness. . . . What does this result from—task cohesion or social cohesion? In units composed of self-selected volunteers, who can definitively say?

Without meaning to, women automatically alter the chemistry in all-male groups.

If one looks closely at what's being written about military cohesion, two things jump out. Social scientists measure cohesion either by observing groups as they perform various tasks or by asking group members to rate their own sense of their unit's performance and the strength of their attachments to it. No one asks soldiers to map their attachments to one another. Nor does anyone examine group dynamics over time. As a consequence, the way cohesion works, what makes it work—who belongs, who doesn't, and why—can't be either measured or described. Yet chemistry matters, more perhaps than anything else.

Consider the following list of what a medical task force is said to need in order to stay cohesive: leadership, meaningful work, the means to cope with boredom, and confidence that family members will be taken care of at home. Say the unit happened to be all-male. Would the introduction of women create problems in any of these spheres? Clearly not.

Now consider this same set of criteria for a Special Forces or Sea, Air, Land (SEAL) team. Just training for combat adds new pressures. Operational intimacy is one. Few sets of Americans experience the enforced togetherness that combat soldiers do. Prisoners might come close. But even overcrowded jails don't impel men to coordinate their every waking moment, as is required in a hide site or foxhole.

Under such conditions there is only one real keeper of order: intimacy can't be a prelude to sex. And it won't be—as long as heterosexual men are kept separated from women. At present, teammates always know where they stand with one another, which is on the nonsexual side of intimacy.

As heterosexuals this is not the side of the line they want to stay on with women. Or, to paraphrase what one former Special Forces soldier has been telling me for years, "Men don't sit across from teammates and think about sleeping with them."

An unresolvable problem: sexual attraction

Ultimately, this is the basic, undeniable, unresolvable problem: heterosexual men like women in ways they don't like other men. What they feel for women is not what they feel for men. How they think about women is not how they think about men. And what they see when they look at a woman is not another man.

> As one officer and gentleman explained to me several years ago: If a woman comes into my office, I do a physical assessment. Even if it's just ten seconds, I go through a sexual scenario with that woman. Can I ignore it? I try to. In this culture, there are penalties for acting that out. But it's natural. There's nothing wrong with it. We have to be real about it.

Indeed. His remarks have since been seconded by numerous other men of all ranks who, on their own, would never admit they mentally disrobe women. Nor from watching them would women be any the wiser, though men don't have to—and decidedly don't—hide from each other the extent to which they fantasize about women. Instead, they embellish, edit, discuss, and then compare notes.

In fact, a graphic fascination with women may be the only thing all heterosexual men share, which is one reason females are talked about the way they sometimes are. If everyone in a group fished, fishing might serve a similar purpose, since anyone telling a fish story is expected to exaggerate, brag, and lie. But talking one-sidedly about sex works better still because it allows men who already know everything there is to know about one another's physical capabilities to engage in one-upsmanship without anyone present being able to prove them wrong. Given that some amount of posturing is critical to bonding—to prove who belongs, who doesn't, and why—the trick for combat units is to have something over which soldiers can compete without this jeopardizing unit integrity. Ergo the inexhaustible usefulness of real and imagined relationships with women.

Make those women real, though, and what had been benign posturing turns into serious competition. Worse, the fact that women pay special attention right back only further strains relations among even the closest friends.

Without meaning to, women automatically alter the chemistry in all-male groups. As soon as the first soldier acts protective, defensive, flirtatious, or resentful, he initiates a dynamic which causes others to do the same, to do the opposite, or to do something else all in the name of setting themselves apart. This is completely antithetical to what units need, which is for individuals to work together and not at cross-purposes. Nor is the rivalry just over who's paying how much attention to whom. It is also about whether special attention should be paid at all. Even for those who are convinced that females shouldn't be treated any differently from males, there's a problem. To ensure that women aren't receiving any extra attention requires paying special attention.

To a greater and different degree than any other type of organization, small combat units are predicated on complementarity and unquestionable mutual trust. To achieve this requires, first, an all-for-one, one-for-all ethos. Second, responsibilities, dangers, and rewards must be shared. Third, what there is to be shared must be literally shared. If, for instance, there is food to be had, everyone eats. The same goes for sex. If there is sex to be had, then anyone who wants it should be able to get it. If not, tension mounts.

Nowhere else does teamwork demand these same sorts of commitments, and the reasons why there can be no exclusive relationships should be obvious—to prevent envy, frustration, impatience, inequity, disgust. Without question, lust poses the most immediate threat. But love may actually be worse. Love rearranges loyalties. It binds one pair of individuals more closely to one another than to anyone else. The good-of-the-group shrinks to two. Just the intimation that two out of six or ten or twelve individuals have found, or are on the verge of finding, everything they need in one another subverts the raison d'etre of a combat unit, which is to return to loved ones, to comfort, and to safety only after the mission is complete. With women present, the potential for love being fulfilled, as well as lust requited, lurks.

The goal should be that the US military remain strong enough . . . not to have to . . . [recruit women into combat positions].

But present or absent, and despite graphic banter, women never mean only sex to soldiers. Rather, they represent a contradictory bundle of things, and when absent what they evoke includes home, family, the future, and everything that's worth fighting for—nonviolence especially.

Truth be told, men are more dependent on women than they often dare admit. Soldiers in combat seem especially dependent. We see this over and over again in written memoirs, and can hear it in veterans' accounts. It's revealed in the fact that mail matters, in the photos soldiers cherish, in the ways memories and dreams sustain them. This is perhaps best captured recently by Tom Hanks' character in the film *Saving Private Ryan*. Being able to picture his wife at home in her rose garden not only kept Captain Miller sane, but noble.

Combat soldiers' mental health may well depend on their having such a contrast to draw. On the one hand, there is the horrific world in which they're mired. On the other, there is the far more ideal world which places women above the fray. In combat nothing is clear-cut. No participant ever knows when he might be killed, maimed, spattered with gore, rescued, or relieved. All the more reason, then, to treat the idea of women—girlfriends, wives, mothers, sisters, daughters—as sacrosanct. Women as succor (and sanity) to return to provides something for soldiers to live for beyond honor, duty, and the filthy, smelly, foul-mouthed males beside them. With women right there, "women" as an ideal would never work.

This may be reason enough to keep females out of foxholes. But that is only if we are willing to pay veterans' experiences their due.

What don't we already know?

Curiously, experience seems to count for little in the women-in-combat debate. The fact that only combat soldiers and combat veterans know what comprises cohesion in combat units doesn't seem to rate. Nor does the fact that men already know how women's presence would affect them. For instance, one argument advanced for integrating women into combat units is that prior to desegregation white soldiers feared that integrating blacks into their units would destroy cohesion, just as men (black and white) now argue women will. But no matter how vigorously critics of the combat exclusion laws make this case, the analogy is wrong. Segregation kept the races apart prior to integration; soldiers of all colors are raised by women, grow up with women, attend school with women, woo women, marry women, and remain keenly interested in women. And though they may not always understand women (as so much of our popular culture contends) they know they are attracted to them. Attraction was hardly the reason whites who opposed integration fought to keep blacks out.

[Men] know they can't always trust themselves. . . . This unspoken truth is reason enough to keep combat units from being mixed.

Nor is this the only selective editing being done. Scholars often refer to the fact that women have successfully fought alongside men in such disparate locales as Greece, the Soviet Union, Israel, Vietnam, and Eritrea, as if this evidence of women's presence on the battlefield is proof that they can be present with no ill effects. Surely, in a war of national survival, in a war fought on American soil, American women, too, might be pressed into service. But the goal should be that the US military remain strong enough for this not to have to occur. Nor is there any suggestion that if sufficient men had been available in any of these other countries, women would have been sent to the front at all. In fact, the Liberation Tigers of Tamil Eelam (LTTE), famous for their discipline and the prominent role of female soldiers today, deploy women only because they lack sufficient numbers of male recruits. In doing so, though, they've also had to sacrifice one of their most legendary fighters; in order to try to make the rule against liaisons stick, he and his lover—a female soldier—were publicly executed. It's hard to imagine our military being able to avail itself of the same technique.

If much has been made of exceptional situations, much has likewise been made of individual females who have found, or fought, their way into combat. American women inadvertently caught in firefights during our incursions in Panama and the Gulf have been regarded as pioneers and depicted as heroes. Praise has been heaped on their coolheadedness and professionalism, which have been offered up as proof that women can handle themselves fine. But fine in what? In limited engagements? What should be the threshold for proof?

Perhaps it shouldn't be combat at all. Unless we are willing to bet that all future wars will be counted only in hours, combat units will face long periods of boredom in addition to intense bursts of activity. Getting along during lulls may be as important as cohering during combat. It may, in fact, be essential to the group's subsequent ability to operate as an effective, cohesive group. Downtime is frequently treated as playtime. Surely that's necessary, but as [psychologist] Sigmund Freud pointed out almost a century ago, Thanatos and Eros [Greek gods of War and Love] are hard to keep apart. It's far easier when sources of temptation just aren't around.

Meanwhile, though combat is often talked about as the ultimate test of a unit, enforced togetherness will stress bonds too. Confined in close quarters, kept on edge, never quite knowing what will happen next . . . why add the potential for mistrust to so much uncertainty? In some regards, training, which is what our Army spends most of its time doing, may be even more trying. Not only do periods of intense activity puncture long, monotonous routines, but no one's survival is at stake. Thus, affection has plenty of time to build, as do suspicions.

Talk to any soldier who has spent time in a hide site, in a snow cave, or on lonely, boring guard duty. Does he really think it would be possible to lie there, shaking and shivering, waiting in the dark, with a female soldier right beside him, and not have that make some sort of difference? Even if no emotional connection is made, will everyone else realize that? Potential alone is corrosive. Conjecture breeds doubt, doubt suspicion, suspicion mistrust.

And mistrust is infectious. It might even be endemic. What men can't say too loudly is that, when it comes down to it, they know they can't always trust themselves. In the end, this unspoken truth is reason enough to keep combat units from being mixed, and it renders worries over women's weaknesses (whatever they might be) largely irrelevant. It's the vulnerability of men which proves the real stumbling block. Not only are men weak when it comes to women, they're partial too. This isn't just elemental; it's immutable.

Proceed with caution

Ironically—and unfortunately, given the gravity of this debate—men who are direct, blunt, and even brutal with each other can't be so forthcoming with women about the various kinds of attraction females qua females hold. That's not how the minuet between the sexes works. But unless men are more frank, unless they make clear to women what's so obvious to them, those who advocate integrating women into their units will be able to continue to assume that with just a bit more time and pressure, with just a few more enlightened males having attained positions of power, and once better legal briefs are filed, women will have to be accepted in SEAL platoons, on SF teams, and throughout the combat arms. If only the advocates understood such units better. Then they might recognize their decisive error—that acceptance is not belonging. Tolerance is not what impels a combat unit to do the impossible. To risk everything together requires unwavering mutual trust.

What might convince lift-the-ban proponents to reexamine their premises? Disinclined as they are to listen to combat veterans and combat soldiers in this country, who are the only experts we have, perhaps they will turn to experts abroad, particularly as the Germans and British abolish their own combat exclusion laws. Perhaps the European experience will shed light on how effective integrated combat units can be. Actually, the fact that it is our allies doing this affords us an unprecedented advantage. We will be able to objectively study the consequences of mixing men and women in combat units. Let mixed units prove themselves to be as capable as single-gender units on the front lines or behind the lines in a long, drawn-out war. And then—but only then—we might consider following suit.

5

Mothers Do Not Belong in the Military

Phyllis Schlafly

Phyllis Schlafly is a syndicated conservative columnist.

The U.S. invasion of Iraq during the spring of 2003 has exposed the military's shameful policy of sending the mothers of infants into battle. Several servicewomen were taken prisoner by the Iraqis; the body of one woman, the mother of two small children, was discovered by troops in a shallow grave. This tragic event is evidence of the military's lack of courage in standing up to militant feminists. Placing women, many of whom are mothers, in dangerous combat situations runs contrary to the importance Americans place on family and motherhood.

The face of war is never pretty, but this time war showed us images we have never seen before. We saw pictures of mothers being sent to Iraq [in the spring of 2003] to fight one of the cruelest regimes in the world.

An assault on family and motherhood

What is the matter with the men of this country—our political and military leaders—that they acquiesce in the policy of sending mothers of infants out to fight [now deposed Iraqi president] Saddam Hussein? Are they the kind of man who, on hearing a noise at 2 A.M., would send his wife or daughter downstairs to confront an intruder?

Three young women were part of the maintenance crew that took a wrong turn and was ambushed by the Iraqis. Shoshana Johnson, fortunately, has been rescued, thanks to an Iraqi who told the Americans where the U.S. prisoners of war (POWs) were hidden.

In the joy of reconciliation, let's not forget the shame on our country that this single mother of a two-year-old baby was assigned to a position where she could be captured. She didn't volunteer to serve in combat; she volunteered to be an Army cook.

Jessica Lynch didn't volunteer for combat either. She wanted to be a

51

kindergarten teacher and joined the Army because jobs were scarce in West Virginia.

Jessica was rescued by U.S. troops thanks to an Iraqi who was disgusted by the way his fellow Iraqis were slapping her around as a wounded prisoner. Even that Iraqi understood that a female POW is different from a male POW.

The third woman, Lori Piestewa of Arizona, didn't make it back alive. Her body was discovered by our troops in a shallow grave.

Let's not forget the shame on our country that [a] single mother . . . was assigned to a position where she could be captured.

Lori was the single mother of a 4-year-old son and a 3-year-old daughter. Did the Iraqi threat to U.S. national security really require those two children to sacrifice their only parent?

The reason these sorry things have happened is that the men in our government and in our military lack the courage to stand down the feminists and repudiate their assault on family and motherhood.

Shoshana, Jessica and Lori were the victims of trickle-down feminism. The female officers (plus the militant feminists who would never serve in the military) demand the "career opportunities" of combat roles, and claim that a servicewoman is fully deployable six months after giving birth, while the privates get the really dangerous assignments.

The pictures of a terrified Shoshana being interrogated by her Iraqi captors and of Jessica carried on a stretcher show the toll on the mothers. How about the costs to the little ones left behind?

The war picture that graphically shows this side of the problem was of an apprehensive two-year-old, Teresa Garcia, hanging on for dear life to the legs of her mother, Army Captain Dorota Garcia, as she stood suited up with rifle and gear, ready to depart for Iraq from Fort Hood, Texas.

The elusive number of mothers at war

Cable television is giving us 24-hour-a-day front-line coverage of the war in Iraq from imbedded and non-imbedded journalists. Funny thing, one statistic is missing from their comprehensive reports.

How many mothers of infants and toddlers (among the 212,000 women in the U.S. military today) are over there in the Iraqi war? How many are single mothers, and how many are married mothers whose husbands are already serving in Iraq, leaving their children parentless at home?

How many are like Army Specialist Tamekia Lavalais, leaving behind her 21-month-old baby whose father is already in Iraq. She said she wouldn't have joined the Army "if I'd known this was going to happen."

The government won't give us the count on mothers, and reporters seem afraid to ask. Is it because that statistic is classified information that would be harmful to national security if the enemy knew it, or because that statistic would be harmful to the reputations of U.S. politicians and generals if the American public knew about our military's anti-motherhood policy?

Or is it because reporters are chicken in the face of the militant feminists? Bernard Goldberg tells in his best-selling book *Bias* that even tough [journalist] Sam Donaldson "turns into a sniveling wimp when it comes to challenging feminists."

The politicians have brought this embarrassment on our nation because they allowed themselves to be henpecked by the militant feminists. The whole idea of men sending women, including mothers, out to fight the enemy is contrary to our belief in the importance of the family and motherhood and, furthermore, no one respects a man who would let a woman do his fighting for him.

Women serve our country admirably, both on the home front and in many positions in the U.S. Armed Forces. But there is no evidence in history for the proposition that the assignment of women to military combat jobs is the way to advance women's rights, promote national security, improve combat readiness, or win wars.

America is alone in this extraordinary social experimentation to send mothers to war. We hope, when the war is over, that the President and the military will change these shameful feminist policies.

6

Servicewomen Are Balancing Family and Military Duties

Faye Bowers

Faye Bowers is a staff writer for the Christian Science Monitor, *a daily newspaper.*

Women's numbers in the active military and the reserves have grown significantly in the past thirty years. During the U.S. invasion of Iraq, begun in the spring of 2003, thousands of women reservists were activated for military duty, leaving behind jobs and families. Interviews with women, their family members, and employers indicate, however, that they are all learning to cope with the women's deployment. Women are using email to keep in touch with their children, husbands are taking on greater domestic roles, and the military is providing support on arranging interim salaries with employers and setting up family benefits.

Staff Sergeant Martha Sass, her five children, and her husband cried for two straight days one week after the 9/11 attacks—when she got orders to ship out.

Lieutenant Commander Tara McFeely's new clients were crestfallen in September 2002 when she told them she had to leave for a year, possibly two, after receiving mobilization orders just two months into her job as an international-security consultant.

Women called to duty

As the US ratchets up deployment of troops, a growing number of women reservists are being called to active duty—and being asked to create family-contingency plans and put other careers on hold.

Women's numbers in both the active military and reserves have grown in the past 30 years, as policy changes have opened more roles to them. And many women have chosen the reserves—drilling one weekend

Faye Bowers, "'Mom? Telephone for You. It's the Army'; of Reservists Called up so Far, Nearly 20 Percent Are Women—Prompting New Military Measures to Help Families Cope," *Christian Science Monitor*, January 15, 2003. Copyright © 2003 by The Christian Science Publishing Society. Reproduced by permission.

per month—because it's more amenable to families and careers.

Now, though, they are torn between two callings: They've volunteered and are committed to serving their country. At the same time, they have full, demanding lives.

"My oldest daughter was pregnant when I was called up, and stressed out," says Sergeant Sass. "She said, 'Oh no, you're not going to be here for me.'" Though Sass was riddled with guilt, her daughter was fine—as were her husband and four other kids.

Because the increase in women reservists—and their mobilization—is a fairly new phenomenon, it's difficult to gauge the effects of being called to active duty on their families' lives or on their own. But interviews with several women who have been recently mobilized show ways in which they are coping with family and career changes.

Women [reservists] who have been [called to active duty] . . . are coping with family and career changes.

"There are more women in the reserves than ever before, and more women in the reserves than in the active services," says David R. Segal, director of the Center for Research on Military Organization at the University of Maryland. "Deployment has a particular impact on reservists . . . [in] disrupting their normal civilian lives."

And, Professor Segal says, "This is going to be a major change, considering most policymakers are from the Vietnam generation. And during the Vietnam War, we did not make extensive use of the reserves. Joining the reserves then was an honorable way of avoiding wartime service. Now we have designed the force in such a way that we can't go to war without the reserves."

Families and employers learn to adjust

Husbands are taking on greater domestic roles—helping with homework and housework, coordinating soccer carpools, paying bills. Employers are finding ways to fill gaps during absences. And the military is developing support programs to ease the women and their families through deployment.

Sass's family learned to live without her for nearly a year. She received her mobilization call in September 2001. By early October, she was at Incirlik Air Base in eastern Turkey, helping coordinate medical evacuation flights for soldiers who'd been wounded in the war in Afghanistan, as well as for prisoners who were detained in Afghanistan and later sent to Guantanamo Bay.

Women reservists are needed for such jobs—roles that aren't critical in peacetime, but are crucial in war.

The Pentagon increased its deployments to the Persian Gulf by 62,000 in January 2003, bringing the total to about 150,000. At the same time, 57,000 reservists have been activated. Of those, nearly 20 percent are women. And those numbers have more than doubled since 1980.

In Sass's unit, 5 of 18 members, including the commander, were women. She says the unit supported one another through family separations—especially at holidays. When one colleague received a digital movie camera for Christmas, he helped Sass assemble a birthday video for her 13-year-old. That was a huge hit, as were the daily e-mails between her, the other children, and her husband, Benjamin, who'd never used e-mail before. "I think I knew more about them and their daily routines while I was away than when I was at home," she says.

One of the biggest benefits, she recalls, was how close the rest of the family grew in her absence. They spent more time together—especially during Thanksgiving and Christmas—cheering one another up and helping with chores.

She's pleased to report that her family is maintaining those habits, even now that she's back at her civilian job as a training coordinator at the Robert Bosch Corporation, in Charleston, South Carolina.

Commander McFeely says her employer—Booz, Allen, Hamilton—will hold her job for her, too, though she only began last July [2002]. Currently, she works at the Office of Naval Intelligence in Suitland, Maryland, examining the world from a "maritime perspective . . . , poising for a war against Iraq and watching North Korea."

She says she was only slightly disappointed to get the call from the military in September [2002]. "I did this with my eyes wide open," she says, "And I will come back only more qualified to my job."

McFeely's husband has his own business, which has given the couple flexibility. And he understands the military's pull: The two met in the Navy, and he, too, is a member of the Navy reserves.

McFeely says the military is extremely supportive, with advice on arranging salaries—her employer makes up the difference between her salary and what the military pays—as well as writing wills and setting up family benefits.

Support for families

Chief Master Sergeant Marva Harper is an adviser to the commander of the US Air Force's 419th Fighter Wing, based at Hill Air Force Base, Utah. "Last weekend I was a civilian," she laughs.

Now, she's helping roughly 1,000 people with family issues. After four years of active naval duty in the 1960s, she followed her Air Force husband around. Today, they're both in the Air Force reserves. Three of their four children are on active duty; the fourth will attend basic training in April.

She says in 40 years of military life, she's seen many changes—one of the biggest being the growing acceptance of women. Another is how the military has evolved in its family support, on everything from McFeely's benefits advice to who to call if a hot-water heater breaks.

7

The Best Soldier for the Job: A Personal Perspective

Lillian A. Pfluke

Lillian A. Pfluke served in the U.S. Army from 1979 to 1995, reaching the rank of major.

In 1976 the author, a talented female athlete, was recruited to join the first class of women to attend West Point, the U.S. Military Academy outside New York City. She describes the mental toughness required to be a woman in such a male-dominated environment and how her leadership skills and aggressive nature earned her the respect of male peers. Entering the army upon graduation from West Point, she experienced increasing frustration with the army's refusal to open infantry positions to women. She eventually retired from the army in 1995 and has become an outspoken critic of the army's treatment of women, maintaining that, regardless of gender, the army must adopt the simple policy of selecting the best soldier for the job.

When he was ten and I was twelve, my brother John and I were the biggest football fans in the world. We carried a pigskin with us everywhere we went so we could run pass patterns whenever we had a few moments to do so. Pass patterns were especially fun when we could talk Dad into playing quarterback. Dad could throw a lot farther than either one of us, so running a deep fly pattern when Dad put it, up there was the ultimate thrill.

One fall, Dad's boyhood friend talented tomboy Jerry and his wife were visiting us for a few days, and we were showing them around the city. On these tours, when John and I got back to the car before the rest of the family did, we would get the football out and toss it around. Dad and Jerry started throwing the ball around with us as we waited. As the rest of the family caught up and came toward us in the parking lot, Dad let loose with one last bomb. I could tell with a glance that it was long . . . way long. Nonetheless, I took off to try to run under it. With visions of Gene Washington running under a John Brodie pass, I strained to get every bit of speed out of my young legs. I could sense that even a quick look over my shoulder would slow me down too much to make the catch, so at what seemed like the right moment I stretched out my arms and watched with tremendous satisfaction as the ball came down right onto my fingertips. In more than twenty-six years of playing on various athletic teams since then, this still ranks as one of my very best catches ever.

I jogged back toward the car, breathless and grinning from ear to ear. Dad and Jerry were whooping and hollering and slapping each other on the back. John was dumbstruck. As I casually flipped Dad the ball and got in the back seat of the station wagon, I overheard Jerry say something that I didn't think much of at the time but that has come to haunt me recently: "What a waste of talent—too bad she's a girl!"

I . . . went into the Army convinced that if I consistently showed my . . . competence, the barrier against women in combat would fall.

I guess you can tell that I was a tomboy. I was also a great leader from an early age, being the oldest of five children. I've had someone to lead around since I was fourteen months old and my sister Teresa came along, so I have a knack for getting people to do things they may not otherwise want to do. In fact, if you talk to people who knew me in my youth, they'd all tell you the same thing: great student, great athlete, great leader.

One other thing really characterizes me: I hate being told I can't do something because I'm a girl. When my brother John got a paper route I wanted one, too. Unfortunately, the paper didn't want a papergirl. So, I used my then four-year-old brother Paul's name to get the route. I was amused when two years after I started the route, the newspaper finally changed its policy and allowed papergirls. They wrote an article about me as the first new papergirl. I never told them I had had the route all along.

I swam competitively from when I was eight years old. When I got to high school, I wanted to swim for the school. There was no girls team in those days, so along with a few buddies I became one of the first girls on the boys team. I won the junior varsity city championship in the butterfly and freestyle sprint events that first year. There were more write-ups in the paper, but again I never understood what the fuss was all about. Of course girls could compete with boys. Why not?

Entering the military

When I was a senior in high school, a West Point [U.S. Military Academy near New York City] recruiter came around to the swim team looking for smart, athletic girls to be in the first class of women. I had never heard of West Point. In my nonmilitary family way out in California, it just never came up. I was definitely intrigued. Shooting guns and jumping out of airplanes sounded like a lot more fun than just studying engineering at the University of California. The further I got through the application process, the more I became convinced that this was for me. I love challenges, and this sounded like a great one.

I was accepted and entered the U.S. Military Academy in the first class of women on 7 July 1976. My family was very proud and supportive because they understood me and my need to do something like this. In fact, the whole family (parents, five kids, and a dog) drove from San Francisco to New York in our van to drop me off.

It certainly was a challenge—and I loved every minute. Pushing myself to physical exhaustion, withstanding all the mental and emotional pressures, inspiring others to push themselves as hard as they could; it was all very fulfilling.

All, that is, except for the fact that I never seemed to get a fair shake. Sure, everyone expects to get harassed as a plebe, but we women all seemed to get more than our share. It's no secret that we were regularly called bitch, whore, and worse; that we were accused of sexual promiscuity or lesbianism; that we were subjected to such inappropriate "pranks" as shaving cream filled condoms in our bed or semen in our underwear drawer. What most people don't realize is the toll that juvenile and hateful treatment takes on a person after a while. The constant barrage of insults, harassment, and inequities made even the strongest among us harbor self-doubts. We all felt very isolated and defensive as a result of never being accepted as contributing members of the institution, and we became extraordinarily sensitive to all issues of prejudice.

[Women] were a separate class of soldier, able to endure all the risks and hardships of Army life but unable to reap the benefits.

During my four years at West Point, I found that infantry training gave me the most personal satisfaction and seemed to be what I was best at. I relished the unique combination of mental and physical toughness required and sought out all of the infantry training experiences available to me, including the Jungle Operations Training Course in Panama, and the Airborne school at Fort Benning. And as an instructor of the challenging Recondo Course at West Point. I loved the intense physical demands, being outside, braving the elements, carrying everything I needed on my back, and finding my way in the woods. I especially enjoyed pushing myself to my personal physical limits. I enjoy risk, challenge, and adventure, and that is what the infantry offers.

Denied an infantry position

In December of 1979, I wrote a letter to Secretary of the Army John O. Marsh requesting an exception to the combat-exclusion policy and expressing my desire to choose infantry as a branch. I was denied, of course, but went into the Army convinced that if I consistently showed my physical, mental, and emotional competence, the barrier against women in combat would fall, as had other barriers for me. I did have a court action lined up with the American Civil Liberties Union Women's Rights Project, but that fizzled when the male-only draft registration legislation passed at the same time as my graduation.

I went into the Ordnance Corps for two reasons. First, it was where I could best use my mechanical engineering education. Second, it was always close to the action. After my four years at West Point, I spent six of my fifteen years in the Army in troop units running maintenance facilities where we fixed tanks, trucks, howitzers, guns, and everything else necessary for a combat division. Army life was fun! It's a real thrill to lead soldiers. To be part of a trained and smoothly functioning team is very fulfilling, especially when it is so because of your efforts.

All throughout those fifteen years, though, my goal was still to prove my competence to get into the infantry: to become an Airborne Ranger and an Infantry battalion commander. Unrealistic expectations? I didn't think so. The entire West Point experience and subsequent socialization into the Army stressed my goals as laudable and important milestones to a successful Army career. After all, for years every single role model I was exposed to in key senior leadership positions wore combat arms brass, airborne wings, and a Ranger tab. . . . I didn't set out to be a maverick; I merely bought into the system and the institutional values as presented.

So, prove my competence I did. I was a physically fit and mentally tough leader of soldiers. I was the National Military Triathlon Champion, the two-time National Military Cycling Champion, the two-time Interservice European Ski Champion. I played rugby. I achieved a maximum score on every Army PT test taken in fifteen years of service. I achieved a First Class score on the U.S. Marine Corps men's PT test. I got a master's degree in mechanical engineering, and years of perfect efficiency reports. I made almost two hundred freefall parachute jumps. I was physical, aggressive, and very competitive. I was a leader who could inspire people to their own personal bests by providing a powerful example and through my genuine infectious enthusiasm for adventure and challenge. Men followed me, bonded with me, respected me, and we fought as a team.

I was also absolutely consistent and outspoken about my views on women in the Army and their lack of opportunity. It was such a gnawing frustration for me to see wonderfully competent women not get taken seriously because of the restrictions on our utilization. We were a separate class of soldier, able to endure all the risks and hardships of Army life but unable to reap the benefits. So, I wrote about these inequities, and talked about them, and confronted my senior leaders about them. I quickly became an "expert," but, more important, an active-duty soldier willing to speak out on the record—a rarity in the Army because a strong part of the institutional culture is to be a team player and not "rock the boat." I wrote opinion pieces and did radio, television, and print interviews. Whenever the subject of Army women was in the news, so was my name.

The best soldier for the job

Because of my notoriety, I was very close to the action as the Army leadership once again debated what to do about "the woman problem in 1993–1995. The actions and attitudes of the senior Army leadership" in that time frame regarding the Army's women's-assignment policy were extraordinarily disheartening and deeply personally disappointing to me.

I had invested nineteen years proving my competence in the organization and suddenly realized that it was *not* a matter of competence. The Army was content to choose less qualified men over more qualified women for its key leadership positions because of politics and deeply entrenched and dated attitudes. In fact, it was fighting desperately for the ability to continue to do so.

As I approached consideration for lieutenant colonel, I realized that my personal ambitions of being an Airborne Ranger and an Infantry battalion commander had slipped away. Since my hope for the institution was stalemated and my personal goals were unrealizable, I reluctantly concluded that with them went my reasons for staying in the Army. I wanted to play on the varsity team and be a contributing member of the first string. I did not want to be tucked away in some support role. I retired on 30 September 1995.

My transition to civilian life went smoothly. With two sons (then three and five years old) and an overseas move when my husband was assigned to France, I had no time to dwell on my disappointment. I started teaching at the French War College, traveled all over Europe, spent more time with my kids, and stayed in great shape. My boys think everyone's mother can do nineteen pull-ups, run faster than Dad, and jump out of airplanes on weekends.

I am still actively engaged in the cause of women in the Army and find that I can speak much more freely about Army women's issues now than I could while in uniform. As I look back on the twenty years since I entered West Point, I take tremendous pride in knowing that I played a role in the vast strides that Army women have made in that time frame. I am confident that the current fusses involving military women (pregnancy rates, sexual harassment, fraternization, deployment issues, and so on) are all just growing pains and transitional problems that will get better as more and more women rise through the ranks. I am convinced, however, that the issues will never go away until the Army adopts one simple policy: The best soldier for the job.

8

Women Should Be Required to Register for the Service Draft

Cathy Young

Cathy Young is cofounder of the Women's Freedom Network, a forum for moderate feminists. She writes a column that appears regularly in the Boston Globe.

A January 2003 lawsuit challenging the federal law that only men are required to register with the Selective Service for a possible military draft has raised questions of fundamental fairness. Although women now serve in positions closer to the front lines of battle than ever before, feminists who champion women in the military maintain that women, unlike men, should be given a choice as to whether they wish to serve in combat. This reasoning, symbolized by male-only draft registration, reinforces longstanding attitudes that men's lives are more disposable and that women must be protected from harm. In the interest of equal citizenship and fundamental fairness, the courts should reject male-only draft registration.

The . . . war with Iraq has sparked a discussion of the possibility of bringing back military conscription. So far, such a move seems unlikely; the only calls for a reinstatement of the draft have come from war opponents such as representative Charles Rangel, Democrat of New York, who argues that war requires "shared sacrifice" (and believes that if a draft were in place, our government would be more reluctant to go to war). But the debate about the draft raises a long-overdue question: What about women? Several young people in Massachusetts have confronted this issue head-on. In January 2003, 18-year-old Samuel Schwartz of Ipswich, aided by his father, civil rights attorney Harvey Schwartz, filed a lawsuit in a federal district court in Boston challenging all-male Selective Service registration as unconstitutional. He has been joined by his 17-year-old sister and two male friends.

Options without obligations

All-male draft registration is an issue that has received little attention—surprising since it is the only instance in which federal law explicitly treats men and women differently. In 1981, the year after mandatory selective service registration for males was reinstated, the Supreme Court upheld the constitutionality of the law on the grounds that the purpose of the draft was to send soldiers into combat, from which women were barred.

In 2003, the legal and cultural landscape is very different. There are far more women in military ranks, doing a far wider variety of jobs—including some combat-related ones. In the 1990 Gulf War [U.S.-led expulsion of Iraq from neighboring Kuwait], women were closer to the front lines than ever before, and were among the casualties of war. Today, women can pilot combat aircraft, serve on combat ships, and command battalions in combat areas. They are still barred, however, from direct engagement with enemy forces on the ground.

Male-only draft registration . . . is a symbol of the longstanding attitude that men's lives are more "disposable."

Curiously, the debate about women in combat has been framed primarily as a debate about women's rights. Feminists who champion women in the military generally talk about giving women the choice to serve in combat, and talk about career opportunities that servicewomen are denied because of the combat exclusion. Men—those who volunteer for service under the present system, and possibly all military-age men if a draft is reinstated—can be required to fight and risk their lives. A young man who does not register for Selective Service theoretically risks prosecution, and forgoes a chance for a student loan.

This paradox has led men's advocates such as author Warren Farrell to charge that feminism seems to give women options without obligations. Male-only draft registration, he argues, is a symbol of the longstanding attitude that men's lives are more "disposable" and that women must be protected from harm.

Indeed, some of the opposition to drafting women and putting them on the front lines is explicitly rooted in this chivalrous mentality. In the book *The Kinder, Gentler Military*, Stephanie Gutmann warns against trying to override the "natural law" that makes men want to protect women and makes societies reluctant to send women to die on the battlefield. Meanwhile, contemporary feminist dogma, fixated on male violence against women, largely avoids confronting the fact that especially in the West, patriarchy has involved not only women's oppression but women's protection.

Those feminists who have honestly confronted this issue have a point when they argue that chivalry is infantilizing. It's no accident that the claim for special protection lumps women with children. In a culture that has rejected the belief that "natural law" relegates women to subordination in marriage and exclusion from public life, public policy rooted in the notion that women's lives are more precious than men's is unconscionable.

But the combat exclusion is also rooted in practical considerations. Some leading proponents of women's full integration into the armed services, such as retired Air Force Major General Jeanne Holm, remain skeptical about putting women into physical combat—primarily because it requires levels of physical prowess most women don't have. Even the weight of the equipment soldiers in ground combat must carry poses a problem for women.

Most military service, however, does not involve direct engagement with the enemy. In Israel, women are currently drafted but serve in noncombat positions. It should be up to the military, based on the needs of national defense, to decide in what capacity women can be best employed. In the meantime, the courts should reject male-only draft registration as incompatible with equal citizenship.

9

Women Should Not Be Required to Register for the Service Draft

Kathleen Parker

Kathleen Parker is a syndicated journalist whose column appears in more than three hundred newspapers and journals nationwide.

Proponents of requiring women to register with the Selective Service for a possible military draft are misguided. The purpose of a draft is to create a combat-ready force, and since women are not permitted to fight in direct combat, a female draft would be irrelevant. Only if the draft is reconfigured to encompass non-combat roles should women be required to register. Such a reconfiguration would take into account the biological differences between men and women that render women physically unqualified for combat service.

No American war is complete without the Gender Equality Question: Should women be drafted? I feel like filling my remaining column space with "blah blah blah" and taking the rest of the day off. Haven't we figured this one out yet?

A female draft is irrelevant

Apparently not. Angry men weary of being feminized want women, specifically members of NOW (National Organization for Women), to be on the front lines. And feminist-equality advocates, such as [*Newsweek*] columnist Anna Quindlen, think their daughters, not just their sons, should have to register with the Selective Service for a possible draft.

Writing in *Newsweek* [November 5, 2001] Quindlen decried the usual anachronistic arguments against drafting women for military duty: that women would spoil esprit de corps, aren't physically strong enough, would distract male soldiers and would get raped as prisoners of war. It's only fair, she said.

Never mind that all of these arguments happen to be *true*—though admittedly, some women are less distracting than others—it is simplistic to suggest that failing to draft women is "unfair." To whom, our enemies? You can imagine the Taliban's [deposed Islamic fundamentalist regime in Afghanistan] response: "By all means, send us your women. We love shooting women!"

Since women aren't permitted to fight in direct combat, a female draft is irrelevant.

The reason women aren't required to register with the Selective Service is because the purpose of a draft, as currently conceived, is to create a combat-ready force. Since women aren't permitted to fight in direct combat, a female draft is irrelevant.

Quindlen argues that women served in the 1991 Persian Gulf war and that even now female pilots are dropping bombs on Afghanistan. In other words, girls should be required to sign up. But there's a difference between dropping bombs from an airplane, where quick reflexes and mental dexterity are the soldier's tools, and navigating rugged terrain carrying heavy packs, guns and ammo.

On the other hand—and this may be what Quindlen meant but didn't say—there are lots of important non-combat roles women can play in service to their country. So maybe the question needs to be rephrased and the purpose of the draft redefined.

If the draft were reconceived to create a smarter, not necessarily combat force, then women should be included. That's fair because in noncombat roles, most men and most women are more or less equal. In demanding physical contests, with rare exceptions they're not. Thus, pitting women against men in battle is *not* "fair."

I was chatting a few days ago with one of my son's teachers, a young woman in her late 20s. She recently had watched "Saving Private Ryan" and, in the context of our current war, she said, "I don't think I could do that. I mean, what about all those days when you've got, you know, PMS [premenstrual syndrome]?"

Biology matters

We laughed, but it's not really funny. Of course, we don't like to mention the unmentionable in these discussions. Suggesting that a woman's menstrual cycle might interfere with good soldiering will get you strafed by the feminist phalange, but honest women and men who live with women know better. Biology matters.

Fundamentally, the gender equality question is misplaced in wartime, and we run the risk of being stupider than usual if we aren't vigilant. It's too easy to embrace the argument that because women and men have reached parity in other institutions, they should be treated equally by the military. It's too easy to suggest, as Quindlen does, that military inequality is tantamount to embracing the Taliban's codification of gender fear and ignorance.

The truth is that men and women, though equal under the law, are not the same. Can you believe I have to explain this? My brother and I were from the same litter and were reared under the same household laws, but we weren't, I promise, the same. He was a big, mean, fighting-machine Marine who found Vietnam rather relaxing compared with home; I was a twig-sized girl with a propensity for rescuing insects, and I wouldn't have lasted a day in combat.

Fairness, meanwhile, means divesting oneself of personal interest (feminist theory) and considering the larger picture (staying alive). If we want a combat-ready military force capable of meting out justice to bin Laden and the Taliban, let's leave Britney, Kimberly and Muggins at home.

Not that we really have to concern ourselves. Were Congress to enact a female draft, the post–World War II baby boom would look like a puddle next to the ensuing obstetrical tsunami. America suddenly would be awash in single, 18 year old mothers.

Biology not only matters, it rules; and pregnant women don't do war very well.

10

Military Colleges Should Expel Pregnant Students

Kathryn Jean Lopez

Kathryn Jean Lopez is a reporter for National Review Online, *a Web site of conservative commentary affiliated with the weekly* National Review *magazine.*

A feminist group announced their outrage in January 2002 over a pregnancy policy adopted by the Virginia Military Institute (VMI), a military college in Lexington, Virginia, which began accepting women in 1997. According to the policy, female, as well as male, cadets who choose to marry or become parents must resign from VMI. The policy reinforces the accountability of cadets and ensures their undivided commitment to their duties and responsibilities at VMI. The feminist attack on this policy misses the point that if coed military schools are to be successful, special exceptions cannot be made for female cadets.

[I]n January 2001] the National Women's Law Center, a feminist nonprofit, announced their outrage over a new pregnancy policy at the Virginia Military Institute (VMI).

Addressing the coed reality

According to the new rules, "a VMI cadet who chooses to marry, or to undertake the duties of a parent (including causing a pregnancy or becoming pregnant by voluntary act)" will be expected to resign as a student at the school or will be subject to expulsion. While it's always been forbidden to marry as a student at VMI, the parenthood rule is new. Students also must now sign an annual statement agreeing to abide by the policy.

The policy addresses the reality of a coed VMI, now in its fifth year. Last winter a junior cadet became pregnant. She completed the semester and has not returned (by choice). The school's Board of Visitors passed a resolution last spring instructing VMI's superintendent, Josiah Bunting, to write a policy "whereby a VMI cadet who chooses to marry or to undertake the duties of a parent, by that choice, chooses to forego his or her commitment to the Corps of Cadets and his or her VMI education."

The National Women's Law Center, a non-profit feminist legal group, warns that the policy is sex discrimination and should be repealed immediately, or VMI will wind up back where the feminists took them in 1989—to court. (In 1997, the Supreme Court ruled that the Virginia Military Institute, which is a publicly supported school, had to admit women.)

But the "new" policy may just work (the new aspects are the written agreement and the parental, not just marital, obligations). Just ask Ben Ashmore. He had to leave VMI, giving up his free financial ride, under the marriage-prohibition rules—which have always been in effect—and he's glad he did.

Any woman . . . who insists that pregnancy . . . should not bar them from remaining at VMI [Virginia Military Institute], ought to reconsider why they are there in the first place.

Ashmore was a cadet at the Virginia Military Institute in January 1996 when his high-school sweetheart and fiancee, who was back home in Michigan, called to tell him she had gotten pregnant during his Christmas furlough.

For Ashmore, military life had been a dream since childhood. He knew he wanted to serve in the military after graduation. But after a few days of considering his options, Ashmore quit VMI.

Ashmore knew other guys at VMI who had pregnant girlfriends, wives, and kids. It wasn't allowed, but they managed it. They'd live nearby, and the students would visit them on weekends. "It would have been the easiest course of action," Ashmore remembers—but he knew it was wrong. He wasn't overjoyed, but he resigned his scholarship.

And now, two kids later, and happily married to the same woman he left VMI for, he is quick to defend VMI's policy.

Maintaining standards

"Everything at VMI is based on accountability," Ashmore says. "Young men and women know this before attending. The 'Rat Line' (what the first year is referred to) is designed to instill the highest level of accountability, in every area of a cadet's life." And accountable is what he was when he resigned from VMI, he says—accountable both as a parent and as a cadet. The only way he could see his family, if his girlfriend moved to Lexington, would be only a few hours a week and on Sundays, or illegally. That's no way to be a father, "Not being accountable as a father would have been just as bad as not being accountable in my cadet duties, which would mean that I learned nothing" from VMI.

Funny thing is, Ashmore and the feminists who disagree with him could easily find themselves at the same cocktail parties. Ashmore worked last year as a policy adviser on the Gore/Lieberman campaign in Michigan. He is on the board of directors of the Michigan ACLU. Ashmore even takes up the feminists' concerns: While vehemently endorsing VMI's new official policy, he also cautions them to ensure it is gender-blind in enforcement—since, as he says, it's harder to find the men who get women pregnant than it is to find women who are pregnant.

If a coed military, and coed military schools are to be successful, standards must remain the same. VMI has been unrelenting on this count. Before launching lawsuits, the National Women's Law Center ought to get a lesson on the essence of VMI from Mr. Ashmore. And any woman—or man—who insists that pregnancy, or the behavior that leads to pregnancy, should not bar them from remaining at VMI, ought to reconsider why they are there in the first place.

11

Military Colleges Should Not Expel Pregnant Students

Marcia D. Greenberger and Jocelyn Samuels

Marcia D. Greenberger is copresident of the National Women's Law Center (NWLC), an organization that seeks to protect the educational and workplace rights of women. Jocelyn Samuels is the vice president and director of education at the NWLC.

A policy adopted by the Virginia Military Institute (VMI), a coed military college in Lexington, Virginia, expels cadets who marry or become pregnant. This policy unfairly targets female students and is in violation of federal and state law. Title IX of the Education Amendments of 1972 bars discrimination on the basis of sex in educational institutions receiving federal financial assistance. The Fourteenth Amendment to the U.S. Constitution and Virginia's Human Rights Act both prohibit discrimination based on sex and pregnancy. Further, prior to its admission of women, VMI ignored and refused to penalize male cadets who fathered children. VMI's current policy singles out female cadets who become visibly pregnant; meanwhile, the policy contains no mechanism for confirming that male cadets have become parents.

The National Women's Law Center is a non-profit organization working to protect the rights and opportunities of women and girls in education, the workplace and other aspects of their lives. We write concerning a parenting policy at the Virginia Military Institute ("VMI") that violates the rights and equal educational opportunities of female students, and request that you rescind this policy immediately.

Unfairly targeting pregnant students

As you know, VMI's Board of Visitors last year directed you to adopt a regulation "whereby a VMI cadet who chooses to marry, or to undertake the duties of a parent (including causing a pregnancy or becoming pregnant by voluntary act)," will be expected to resign or will be expelled from

Marcia D. Greenberger and Jocelyn Samuels, "Letter to Major General Josiah Bunting III of the Virginia Military Institute, January 14, 2002," www.nwlc.org, 2002. Copyright © 2002 by the National Women's Law Center. Reproduced by permission.

VMI. VMI has now proposed a regulation to implement this policy. The regulation states that "absent voluntary resignation, should [VMI] confirm that a cadet is married or the parent of a child, such cadet shall be separated from the Corps, for failure of eligibility, at the end of the semester in which the information is received and confirmed." We understand that the regulation is effective as of today, January 14, 2002.

Because they unfairly target and burden pregnant students, the parenting provisions of both the resolution adopted by the Board of Visitors and the implementing regulation (hereinafter the VMI "policy") constitute sex discrimination in violation of federal and state law. Title IX of the Education Amendments of 1972 ("Title IX"), bars discrimination on the basis of sex in educational institutions that receive federal financial assistance. The 14th Amendment to the United States Constitution similarly bans sex discrimination, as well as the application of arbitrary presumptions about an individual's capabilities. And Virginia's own Human Rights Act prohibits discrimination based on sex and pregnancy, among other bases, and invalidates conduct that violates federal law.

Because they unfairly target and burden pregnant students, [VMI's parenting policies] . . . constitute sex discrimination.

The sex discrimination prohibitions of Title IX indisputably cover discrimination based on a woman's pregnancy. *See, e.g., Pfeiffer v. Marion Center Area School District*, 917 F.2d 779, 784 (3d Cir. 1990) (Title IX regulations bar discrimination based on pregnancy, parental status, and marital status); *Wort v. Vierling*, C.A. No. 82-3169, Order at 6-7 (C.D. Ill. Sept. 4, 1984) (dismissal of student from National Honor Society based on pregnancy violated both Title IX and the Constitution). In fact, the regulations implementing Title IX expressly bar a school from excluding any student from its education program on the basis of pregnancy or related conditions. The regulations further prohibit application of "any rule concerning a student's actual or potential parental, family, or marital status which treats students differently on the basis of sex." VMI's parenting policy directly contravenes these prohibitions; it is a rule about actual or potential parental status that, by its very nature, treats students differently on the basis of sex and that will significantly disadvantage only those students who can become pregnant—that is, female students.

VMI's policy requires the Institute to impose disciplinary consequences on a cadet (unless the cadet has voluntarily resigned) once it has confirmed that the cadet is the parent of a child. Because it is a visible manifestation of a woman's impending parenthood, a female cadet's pregnancy will automatically, and in all cases, trigger application of this rule. By contrast, the policy contains no mechanism for confirming—or even for discovering—that male cadets have become parents. This is fundamental sex discrimination under the terms of Title IX. *Compare Chipman v. Grant County School District*, 30 F. Supp. 2d 975, 979 (E.D. Ky. 1998) (preliminary injunction granted against policy barring those who had engaged in premarital sex from membership in National Honor Society, where policy excluded 100% of "young women who have become pregnant from premarital sex and have become visibly pregnant," and "0% of young men who have had premarital sexual relations"); *Cline v. Catholic Diocese of Toledo*, 206 F.3d 651, 667 (6th Cir. 2000) (under analogous statute, Title VII of the Civil Rights Act of 1964, "a school can not use the mere observation or knowledge of pregnancy as its sole method of detecting violations of its premarital sex policy").

Refusing to penalize male cadets

There is substantial evidence that VMI adopted its policy precisely as a means to exclude pregnant female cadets. Prior to its admission of women—and despite its current claims that men, as well as women, cannot act both as students and as parents at the same time—VMI did not act to expel students based on marriage or parental status. VMI did not enforce its then-existing policy prohibiting cadets from marrying. *See* Chittum, "VMI Drafts Pregnancy Policy," *Roanoke Times*, front page (June 30, 2001) (VMI rule forbidding marriage applied "with a 'don't ask, don't tell' policy"). And it ignored, and refused to penalize, male cadets who fathered children and undertook the duties of fatherhood. *See The Washington Post*, "Pregnant on the Parade Ground" at B08 (April 1, 2001) (citing examples showing that "parenthood has been a fact of life for several VMI cadets in the past few decades"). In fact, the VMI Board of Visitors adopted the current policy only after a female cadet became pregnant while attending the school.

The penalties VMI has adopted further violate Title IX and its implementing regulations. The regulations not only bar exclusion of pregnant cadets, but also require affirmatively that pregnancy be treated "as a justification for a leave of absence for so long a period of time as is deemed medically necessary . . . at the conclusion of which the student shall be reinstated to the status she held when the leave began." We also behave that VMI's policy is inconsistent with the policies adopted at other schools. According to news reports, The Citadel [military college in Charleston, South Carolina], for example, treats pregnancy as a temporary medical disability which may at some point require a medical furlough; the United States Naval Academy [in Annapolis, Maryland,] allows pregnant midshipmen to either resign or to take a leave of up to one year.

> *Prior to its admission of women . . . VMI did not act to expel students based on marriage or parental status.*

VMI's parenting policy also violates the Equal Protection Clause of the 14th Amendment to the United States Constitution. As discussed above, VMI's policy is neither neutral nor justified; it was adopted to, and does, treat female students differently on the basis of sex. There can be no "exceedingly persuasive justification" for this discrimination. *United States v. Virginia*, 518 U.S. 515, 531 (1996). Moreover, to the extent that it creates an irrebuttable presumption that parents cannot meet both their parental and their academic responsibilities, VMI's policy runs afoul of Supreme Court cases requiring an opportunity for individualized consideration of a person's ability or record. *See, e.g., Cleveland Board of Education v. LaFleur*, 414 U.S. 632, 644 (1974) (invalidating "conclusive presumption that every pregnant teacher who reaches the fifth or sixth month of pregnancy is physically incapable of continuing" to teach); *Stanley v. Illinois*, 405 U.S. 645 (1972)(statute containing an irrebuttable presumption that unmarried fathers are incompetent to raise their children violated the Due Process Clause).

Moreover, Virginia's own Human Rights Act makes clear that any conduct that violates a federal discrimination statute will also violate Virginia law. Because VMI's policy, as discussed above, constitutes unlawful discrimination on the basis of sex and pregnancy under federal law, VMI is likely to face liability under state law as well.

VMI's poor approach

Finally, there is nothing in the Order dismissing *United States v. Virginia*, C.A. No. 90-0126-R (Dec. 6, 2001), that sanctions this policy. That Order finds that VMI has met its obligation to "formulate, adopt, and implement a plan that conforms with the Equal Protection Clause of the Fourteenth Amendment as applied to this case by the Supreme Court." As applied by the Supreme Court in the VMI case, of course, the Equal Protection Clause analysis addressed only the admission of women—not the parenting policy VMI has now decided to adopt. And the parties' joint motion to dismiss this case makes explicit that the United States Department of Justice has taken no position on whether VMI's policy complies with either the Equal Protection Clause or Title IX.

For the reasons set forth above, VMI's parenting policy violates the Constitution, the prohibitions of Title IX, and state law. The National Women's Law Center also believes that VMI's approach represents poor policy, in that it may cause young women cadets to seek to terminate their pregnancies in circumstances in which they would not otherwise do so. We urge you to rescind the policy expeditiously and adopt a policy that complies with the law.

We look forward to your prompt reply.

Sincerely,

Marcia D. Greenberger
Co-President

Jocelyn Samuels
Vice President and Director, Education

12

Servicewomen Face Widespread Sexual Harassment

T.S. Nelson

T.S. Nelson is a psychotherapist specializing in sexual trauma recovery. She is the author of For Love of Country: Confronting Rape and Sexual Harassment in the U.S. Military, *from which the following viewpoint is excerpted.*

Surveys conducted by the Department of Defense have confirmed that the sexual harassment of women in the military is a continuing and widespread problem. Seventy-eight percent of women surveyed reported experiencing a behavior consistent with a form of sexual harassment or sexual assault. In addition, one in every twenty-five active-duty women was the victim of rape or attempted rape in the twelve months prior to completing the surveys. Despite congressional and media attention, some branches of the military have tended to minimize or dismiss the issue of sexual harassment and assault against women. A better public and internal understanding of the extent of the problem, however, has prompted stronger disciplinary action against soldiers found guilty of inappropriate behavior.

The problems of sexual harassment and sexual assault in the U.S. military are epidemic. Reports of abuse continue to flood in as the problem continues to emerge. Surveys of women in the military tell a story of rampant sexual abuse and harassment by their male counterparts amid concerns that the issues are being minimized or ignored by military leaders. According to a 1997 article, "Did We Say Zero Tolerance?" in *U.S. News & World Report* ". . . 18 percent of the Army's women say colleagues have tried to coerce them into having sex and 47 percent say they've received unwanted sexual attention." Similarly, a study in 1995 by the Department of Defense (DoD) found that 72 percent of women and 63 per-

T.S. Nelson, *For Love of Country: Confronting Rape and Sexual Harassment in the U.S. Military.* Binghamton, NY: The Haworth Maltreatment and Trauma Press, Haworth Press, Inc., 2002.

cent of men had experienced "sexist behavior" and that 47 percent of women and 30 percent of men received "unwanted sexual attention."

Cause for concern

Each of the service branches has good reason to be concerned about the growing problems of rape and sexual harassment among their ranks. Long before the Tailhook scandal[1] became public knowledge, the Navy Criminal Investigative Services (which includes the Marine Corps) found significant increases in sexual assault cases from 1987 to 1990. Navy authorities were reportedly "concerned about a 55 percent increase in reported rapes at naval bases" (up from 166 in 1987 to 240 reported rapes in 1990). The report also indicated that the Navy was critical of their investigative service for "insensitive treatment of rape victims in many cases."

Despite concerns expressed by Navy officials in 1990, the problem grew significantly worse. According to information provided by the Office of the Undersecretary of Defense, reported rapes jumped from 240 investigated cases in 1990 to 422 in 1992—a nearly 100 percent increase. In 1996, the numbers of reported rapes were nearly identical to four years earlier. Based on these figures very little has changed in the past decade.

Official confirmations of the prevalence of [sexual] abuse [in the military] were . . . acknowledged in . . . two separate Department of Defense surveys.

The Air Force, on the other hand, appears to have taken a more proactive stance over the years with regard to prevention programs for sexual assault and harassment. Nonetheless, the numbers of reported rapes still did not change much over a six-year period according to the Department of Defense statistics provided by the Pentagon. The Air Force had 176 rape report in 1991 and 164 in 1996—only a small change, but the numbers were lower. The biggest difference in the Air Force was in their response to convicted rapists. The average criminal sentence went from 20.28 years in 1991 down to 9 years in 1996. How can the Air Force account for such a dramatic shift in sentencing and punishment for sexual offenders? One would expect the sentencing to increase as public concern and attention to the problem grew.

When the Army found itself in the national spotlight in 1996 with reports of widespread abuse at its training facilities, it took immediate control of the crisis to avert a public relations disaster. The Army held press conferences throughout the investigations, initiated a senior review panel on sexual harassment, conducted studies on sexual assault and gender-integrated training, implemented a toll-free sexual assault hotline, and promptly held court-martials and disciplinary action for all known offenders from the top down.

Nonetheless, despite the Army's efforts, reports of sexual abuse and

1. The Tailhook Association is a private naval aviators organization. At their 1991 convention in Las Vegas, eighty-three women, some of them members of the Navy, were sexually assaulted or harassed by Navy and Marine aviators.

rape by U.S. Army men continued to surface across the globe. The Army hotline was inundated with over 8,000 calls in less than a year's time (of these, 1,360 calls were labeled "actual allegations" by the Army's Department of Public Affairs). In addition to the hotline calls, rape cases that were "officially" reported for investigation to the Army held steady over a six-year time span from 402 reported rapes in 1991 to 440 in 1996 according to Pentagon records.

Not surprisingly, the problem also surfaced with the Department of Veterans Affairs (VA). Ultimately, it is the VA that ends up providing treatment to many of the rape victims years after their discharge from active duty service. According to 1992 testimony before the Senate Veterans Affairs Committee, an estimated 60,000 to 200,000 women veterans were sexually assaulted while on active duty. Clearly, a need exists for such services within the VA due to the high rates of sexual victimization among active-duty service members.

Surveys confirm abuse

Official confirmations of the prevalence of abuse were also acknowledged in at least two separate Department of Defense surveys. The DoD, in conjunction with the Defense Manpower Data Center, conducted one of the largest studies on sexual harassment in the military in 1995. This survey was a follow-up to a similar, earlier study on the same topic in 1988. The 1995 servicewide study on sexual harassment involved three separate surveys. The first survey (Form A, Sex Roles in the Active Duty Military), a replication of the 1988 survey, was a comparison and analysis of improvement over the seven-year time frame. This survey was sent to over 30,000 personnel for a response rate of 46 percent.

The second survey in the 1995 study (Form B, Gender Issues) was sent to over 50,000 service members with a response rate of 58 percent. The questionnaire included items regarding perceptions of the complaint process, reprisals, training, experiences that occurred outside of the work setting, and an expanded list (from the 1988 study) of potential sexually harassing behaviors. In addition, questions were also asked about the service members' perceptions of leadership commitment and efforts to prevent or reduce sexual harassment.

More than three-fourths . . . of women reported experiencing a behavior consistent with a form of sexual harassment or sexual assault.

The last survey in the group (Form C) was sent to 9,856 personnel of which 56 percent participated. This survey was designed to link the results from Forms A and B. It was used "for research purposes" only and was not included in the DoD report made available to the public.

Over 90,000 active-duty men and women worldwide were sent surveys, of which 47,000-plus participated. Respondents were from each of the service branches, including Reserve and National Guard members. Some of the major findings of the 1995 DoD study are summarized here.

. . . The following is what the Department of Defense discovered about the rates of sexual assault and harassment. Note that these rates reflect *only incidents that occurred in the 12 months prior to completing the survey* and do not represent the entire time on active duty.

- Nearly two-thirds (64 percent) of the women surveyed reported experiencing one or more incidents of unwanted, uninvited sexual attention or behaviors at work (1988). In the 1995 study, the numbers decreased to 55 percent of the women.
- For men, 17 percent reported unwanted, uninvited sexual attention or behaviors in 1988, and 14 percent in 1995.
- The list of "uninvited, unwanted sexual attention" on this survey included: actual or attempted rape; pressure for sexual favors; sexual touching; sexually suggestive looks or gestures; letters or materials of a sexual nature; sexual teasing or remarks of a sexual nature; and attempts at involvement with a sexually oriented activity (e.g., group sex or posing nude).

The reported rates of sexual harassment increase substantially when looking at the findings from those who completed Form B. This survey differed from Form A because it included an expanded list of potentially sexually harassing behaviors and specific examples of such. As stated earlier, Form A was a replication of the 1988 survey. Therefore, the extended list in 1995's Form B allowed for a more complete look at the problem.

Sexual harassment is so commonplace that "soldiers seem to accept such behaviors as a normal part of Army life."

The extended list of "unwanted sex-related attention" used on Form B included some of the items from Form A and others such as: display of pornography at the workplace; offensive, sexist remarks; bribes to engage in sex (or offered special favors); sex-related threats or coercion; attempts to kiss or fondle; and attempts to have sex against one's will.

- When given more specific examples of sexual harassment on an expanded list of items, the numbers of respondents reporting such behaviors increased. More than three-fourths (78 percent) of women reported experiencing a behavior consistent with a form of sexual harassment or sexual assault, and 38 percent of the men indicated that they also experienced at least one event in the preceding twelve months.
- The rates of unwanted sexual experiences for men were similar across the services with 39 percent of Army men reporting, and 37 percent reporting from each of the other service branches.
- For women, the rates across the service branches varied significantly: 86 percent of female Marines experienced sexual harassment or sexual assault as compared to 82 percent of Army women; 77 percent in the Navy; 74 percent in the Air Force; and 75 percent in the Coast Guard.

Specific types of sexual harassment were also reported. The following are two key findings in these areas:

- Sexual coercion (e.g., implied job benefits for compliance with or penalties for refusing demands for sex) was reported by more than 10 percent of military women and 2 percent of men.
- Requests or demands for sexual favors were reported by 11 percent of the active-duty women.

The incidence of sexual harassment in the U.S. armed forces is still quite high, even though there was a decline reported from 1988 to 1995. In addition, the reported rates of rape or attempted rape were also significant.

- One in every twenty-five active-duty women (4 percent) and one in 100 military men (1 percent) were victims of rape or attempted rape in the twelve months prior to completing this survey.
- Specifically, 9 percent of women in the Marines, 8 percent of women in the Army, 6 percent of women in the Navy, and 4 percent of women in the Air Force and Coast Guard were victims of rape or attempted rape *in one year alone.*

Abuse makes headlines

Although the Department of Defense had confirmation of the magnitude of the problem some six years earlier, very little was done to effectively remedy a problem that was affecting nearly two-thirds of their female troops and a third of their male troops.

Other studies substantiated the problem as well. Most notably, the Army's Senior Review Panel on Sexual Harassment, the Federal Advisory Committee's Report on Gender Integrated Training and Related Issues, and the General Accounting Office have all assessed the problem.

With the exposure of the intolerable abuse of trainees at Army training installations[2] (namely, but not only, Aberdeen Proving Ground, Fort Leonard Wood, and Fort Jackson) the issue was once again in the news. This time the headlines and the reports captured the attention of Congress. It seemed that everyone was now listening. Senators Olympia Snowe and Charles Robb were interviewed about their response to sexual harassment in the military. The following comments were made by Senator Snowe about this crisis:

> The situation at Aberdeen is quite serious. It is pervasive . . . when consider the fact that you have 50 percent of the drill instructors at Aberdeen under suspension, under question at this point, there may be more.

In agreement, Senator Robb recognized sexual harassment is a problem in society as well as in the military.

It did not take long for the Army to respond to the crisis, not wanting to repeat the mistakes the Navy officials made in their delayed and prolonged response to the Tailhook allegations. Secretary of the Army Togo West developed a senior review panel of retired, active-duty, and senior army officials to study the issue and to report back to him promptly with their findings.

The panel hit an early snag. One of its select members, Sergeant Ma-

2. In 1996 it was revealed that female trainees were forced to have sex with superior officers at several training installations.

jor of the Army, Gene McKinney, was charged with sexual misconduct allegations and released from the panel after the allegations were made public some months later. Despite this disruption, the panel made good on its mission to assess the problem of sexual misconduct and made the report public in the fall of 1997.

The group surveyed and interviewed 30,000 troops at visits to fifty-nine Army facilities worldwide. A surprising and disturbing finding surfaced: 84 percent of women reported they experienced unwanted sexual attention, coercion or assault, yet only 22 percent said they were sexually harassed. This data suggests that there may be some confusion among the troops as to what exactly constitutes sexual harassment. Or is it perhaps that military women have grown accustomed to unwanted sexual innuendoes or behaviors and therefore are not as likely to be offended by the remarks or gestures? Even the Army's review panel discovered:

> Sexual harassment is so commonplace that "soldiers seem to accept such behaviors as a normal part of Army life."

Ignoring the concerns of servicewomen

In the 1997 PBS [public broadcasting] interview, "War on Harassment—Sexual Harassment in the Military," Phil Ponce interviewed members of the Army's Senior Review Panel to address their recent assessment of the problem. Ponce summarized some of the panel's findings including that sexual harassment and sexual discrimination occur throughout the Army and affect both genders, all races, and all ranks. Moreover, Ponce reported that some soldiers do not trust the system, and sometimes they do not trust their leaders with this issue either. . . .

In response to their findings, the panel created 128 recommendations to address the problems of sexual harassment and sexual abuse in the Army. It is unknown as to how many of those recommendations have actually been implemented to date. However, of significant note, the Army's own panel concluded that the service "lacks the institutional commitment" to treat women equally.

The problem of . . . dismissing the issue of sexual harassment and sexual assault against [military] women [has been a longstanding problem].

Despite the sharp criticisms and the carefully developed recommendations from his own senior review panel, Togo West still did not think sexual abuse was endemic in the Army. Once again, the opinions of leadership were not reflective of the concerns of the majority of female members of the Army nor of the general public.

In the extensive PBS series on sexual harassment in the military, Betty Ann Bowser interviewed female soldiers one month after the breaking news about the Aberdeen and Fort Leonard Wood abuses. First, Bowser summarized the magnitude of the issue facing women in the military. She noted that the Army hotline received over 5,000 calls in less than two months—of which 800 calls warranted further investigation. She recalled the Pentagon's own survey just one year earlier when more than half of the military women indicated that they had been sexually harassed while on active duty. Then, she interviewed the group of female soldiers and listened to their perspectives to get a better understanding of the problem. In the process, Bowser discovered "when women were asked to participate in group sessions to talk about sexual harassment, officials said what they heard surprised them."

[Female] employees working at military installations have also found themselves victims of [sexual] abuse.

Despite the facts to the contrary, Army leaders repeatedly misinterpreted or openly denied the pervasiveness of the problem. According to an article in the *Congressional Quarterly Weekly Report* "Army leadership seem to think that most women are happy in the Army despite a 1995 survey showing that less that 50 percent feel their abuse and sexual harassment charges would be taken seriously".

Similar reports of minimizing the problem were noted when Army officials appeared to attribute the complaints of widespread abuse from Aberdeen as a "few bad apples." It was not until the reports escalated and the allegations included other training sites that Pentagon officials reevaluated their initial conclusions.

The problem of minimizing or dismissing the issue of sexual harassment and sexual assault against women occurred long before the news at Aberdeen. According to a February 10, 1997, article from *Feminist News*.

> . . . the Army failed to identity the warning signs of the problem's pervasiveness for over twenty years. In 1980, 150 of 300 women in the 3rd Infantry Division in Germany reported that they were subject to unwanted physical advances. In 1989 and 1996 a majority of women responding to polls conducted in all branches of the military reported that they had encountered some form of sexual harassment. Many of the women also reported that their complaints were met with ridicule and indifference at best and retaliation at worst.

Confounding figures, law reporting rates

The survey findings from 1988 and 1995 are frequently cited since they represent the Department of Defense's best efforts at trying to understand the magnitude of the problem. Although the follow-up survey in 1995 did find that reports of sexual harassment had decreased somewhat, over half of the women in the military still faced sexually abusive behavior on active duty.

The high incidence of sexual victimization is substantiated in other research studies as well. For example, Maureen Murdoch and Kristin

Nichol of the Minneapolis Veterans Affairs Medical Center surveyed women who were being treated at the medical center. Ninety percent of the women in the study, under the age of fifty, were victims of sexual harassment on active duty while 30 percent of the older respondents reported a history of sexual harassment while in the service.

Murdoch and Nichol (1995) found that the incidence of violence against female veterans is much higher than in the general population. They concluded:

> Both domestic violence and sexual harassment while in the military are common experiences for female veterans. Attempted and completed sexual assaults were reported at rates 20 times (higher than) those reported for other government workers.

The DoD released some very different statistics in their annual tracking of reported cases of sexual harassment. *The Washington Times* reported that sexual harassment allegations actually declined in all branches of service except the Navy in 1996. The annual figures revealed that the Navy's sexual harassment complaints increased from 184 to 197 in 1996; the Army's reported cases dropped from 424 to 355; the Marine Corps cases decreased from 96 to 82; and the Air Force also reported fewer cases from the previous year, from 329 to 279 in 1996.

Ironically, only two years earlier, the Department of Veterans Affairs noted that the highest percentage of service women reporting sexual harassment or assault were Gulf War veterans. How is it that the DoD statistics of reported cases are lower than the VA for the same decade? Why is it that so many women (more than half) consistently admit on confidential surveys that they have been victims of sexual harassment or sexual abuse in the military, yet the Department of Defense's official statistics for 1996 show only a few hundred reported cases a year?

The counfounding figures may be due to the fact that the number of rape and sexual harassment victims far exceeds the number of reported cases. This is also true in the civilian sector at the municipal, county, and federal levels. More often than not, victims do not make official reports of sexual violence. The estimates on reporting rape range from 5 percent, to 16 percent, to 32 percent.

Undoubtedly, [more] external oversight [has] prompted a change in the way the military . . . responds to [sexual misconduct].

Rape and domestic violence are known to be the most underreported of all violent crimes, regardless of the jurisdiction. Some of the underlying reasons for the low reporting rates are probably similar for military and civilian victims: fear of the perpetrator, shame and embarrassment, mistrust of the criminal justice system, or a lack of information about the available resources. . . .

The barriers and problems of sexual abuse are not limited to service members. Some civilian employees working at military installations have also found themselves victims of abuse by military personnel. Consider the implications of the following example involving civilians at one military installation.

The New York Times reported that twenty-three civilian, female employees at Fort Bliss, Texas, had filed a class action lawsuit because they stated they were forced to "pose nude and perform sexual acts" while on the job. In one of the cases involving a Fort Bliss Army colonel, the Equal Employment Opportunity Commission recommended the Army pay $300,000 in damages plus medical and legal costs to the sexual harassment victim. The civilian employee alleged that her boss, a colonel in the U.S. Army, threatened her over a six-year period that she would lose her job if she did not submit to his sexual demands. After the Army investigated the allegations, they gave the colonel a letter of reprimand and ordered him to retire early.

In this case, as with many sexual harassment allegations, the Army claims that it is not liable for the colonel's illegal and abusive behavior. Army officials believe they are exempt from liability in part because the victim did not use the established internal procedures for filing her complaint. However, the Supreme Court has ruled that employers can be held liable for their employees' sexually harassing behavior. In such cases, the military is exempt from some of the laws to which other employers must adhere. Debates about jurisdiction, military oversight, and liability are the sources of contention in many sexual harassment and abuse cases.

External oversight prompts change

Reports of sexual misconduct by military personnel against civilian employees, civilians, and other service members are numerous. Many of these allegations spark debate and controversy over how the military is handling such matters. One of the most public investigations of sexual victimization in the military stemmed from the widespread abuse by drill instructors at the previously mentioned Aberdeen Proving Ground in Maryland in 1996. The general public as well as advocacy groups, such as the NAACP (National Association for the Advancement of Colored People), kept a watchful eye on how the military was responding to the allegations.

Undoubtedly, this external oversight prompted a change in the way the military would respond to these issues. Within the first week of the public notification of the allegations, four drill instructors and a captain were suspended and charged, along with fifteen other service men. The Army's hotline was set up immediately to take calls and received nearly 2,000 calls in the first weeks. Army officials noted that over 150 of those initial calls appeared to be credible allegations requiring further investigation.

Finally, by the end of the twentieth century, it seemed as though the public and the Pentagon had a better understanding of the extent of sexual misconduct in the military. This was in part due to the increased publicity regarding rape, abuse, and sexual harassment reports and due to the toll-free hotlines. In addition, allegations came from veterans, retirees, Department of Defense civilian employees, and other civilians—stateside and abroad. As more victims came forward, it seemed as though some of the reported abuses were more incredulous. The following are further examples of the types of harassment and violence committed by U.S. ser-vicemen found on public record.

- At the Air Force Academy, a female cadet in a mock prisoner-of-war camp is urinated on, sexually humiliated, and beaten unconscious.
- Four marines are charged in the rape of a female sailor in Iceland.
- A Naval petty officer from the U.S.S. *Belleau Wood* (a U.S. amphibious assault ship) reportedly molested a Japanese girl in Nagasaki, Japan.
- A female Coast Guard petty officer is threatened with a screw-driver by men who demanded oral sex.
- Two Sea, Air, Land (SEAL) trainees are held for the rape and murder of a Georgia college student.
- A fourteen-year-old American girl was allegedly raped at Kadena Air Force base, Okinawa, by a twenty-four-year-old U.S. serviceman.
- At Annapolis, Maryland, one midshipman twice raped a high school girl and her sister.
- Male trainees are tortured by Marine Corps officers at Camp Leje-une and Camp Smith survival trainings. Their genitals were burned with cigarettes and Tabasco sauce.
- A twenty-four-year-old woman was beaten to death with a hammer by a U.S. serviceman in Japan.

Organizations to Contact

The editors have compiled the following list of organizations concerned with the issues debated in this book. The descriptions are derived from materials provided by the organizations. All have publications or information available for interested readers. The list was compiled on the date of publication of the present volume; the information provided here may change. Be aware that many organizations may take several weeks or longer to respond to inquiries, so allow as much time as possible.

Alliance for National Defense
PO Box 22241, Alexandria, VA 22304
e-mail: ed@all4nationaldefense.org • Web site: www.all4nationaldefense.org

The Alliance for National Defense is an organization that works to promote a full partnership between men and women in the U.S. military, maintaining that such a partnership will strengthen America's national defense. The alliance contends that gender-integrated basic training has been a success. It supports the military's requirement for excellence in performance, regardless of gender, and recognizes the importance of mission accomplishment and combat readiness. The alliance publishes a monthly newsletter in addition to numerous fact sheets and articles available through its Web site.

Center for Military Readiness (CMR)
PO Box 51600, Livonia, MI 48151
(202) 347-5333
e-mail: info@cmrlink.org • Web site: www.cmrlink.org

The Center for Military Readiness is a conservative educational institution created to take a leadership role in formulating military personnel policies. CMR supports equal opportunity for women in the military, but it maintains that training and discipline standards should not be weakened merely to promote the advancement of women, arguing that military readiness will be compromised. It publishes the newsletter *CMR Notes* ten times a year.

Defense Department Advisory Committee on Women in the Services (DACOWITS)
Room 3D769, 4000 Defense Pentagon, Washington, DC 20301-4000
(703) 697-2122
e-mail: dacowits@osd.mil • Web site: www.dtic.mil/dacowits

Established in 1951, DACOWITS is composed of civilian men and women appointed by the secretary of defense to provide policy recommendations on the recruitment, retention, and integration of women in the armed services. In recent years DACOWITS has pushed to open ground- and close-combat assignments, including special operations, to women. As a result, it has come under attack by cultural conservatives who contend that it has introduced "social engineering" into the military. The administration of President George W. Bush has made new appointments to the committee to focus its efforts on a less feminist agenda. DACOWITS publishes biannual reports on issues facing women in the military in addition to research papers and articles.

Heritage Foundation
214 Massachusetts Ave. NE, Washington, DC 20002-4999
(202) 546-4400 • fax: (202) 546-8328
e-mail: pubs@heritage.org • Web site: www.heritage.org

The Heritage Foundation is a conservative think tank that advocates free enterprise and limited government. Heritage researchers maintain that the military has gone too far in promoting women to positions for which they are unqualified. Its publications include the quarterly *Policy Review* and online resources such as *Policy Research & Analysis*, which has featured articles on how gender-integrated basic training has lowered physical standards and damaged the cohesion of training units.

MilitaryWoman.org
e-mail: webmaster@militarywoman.org • Web site: www.militarywoman.org

This Web site serves as a meeting place for women currently serving in the military, female veterans, and women considering a military career. The site posts numerous articles on issues confronting women in the military, including women in combat, military and family life, and sexual harassment.

Minerva Center, Inc.
20 Granada Rd., Pasadena, MD 21122-2708
(410) 437-5379
e-mail: depauw@minervacenter.com • Web site: www.minervacenter.com

The Minerva Center is an educational and research corporation for the study of women in war and women and the military. The center takes a diverse approach to women in the military, covering all aspects of the issue without adhering to a particular political viewpoint. It publishes two periodicals: *MINERVA: Quarterly Report on Women in the Military* and *Minerva's Bulletin Board*.

National Military Family Association (NMFA)
2500 North Van Dorn St., Suite 102, Alexandria, VA 22302-1601
(703) 931-6632 • fax: (703) 931-4600
e-mail: families@nmfa.org • Web site: www.nmfa.org

The NMFA is a nonprofit advocacy group that seeks to improve the quality of military family life by educating Congress, the military community, and the public on the rights and needs of military families. It publishes the monthly newsletter the *Voice for Military Families*, which addresses such issues as the readiness of military mothers for active service and the health care benefits available to their families.

National Women's Law Center (NWLC)
11 Dupont Circle NW, Suite 800, Washington, DC 20036
(202) 588-5180 • fax: (202) 588-5185
e-mail: info@nwlc.org • Web site: www.nwlc.org

The NWLC was founded to protect the legal rights of women in education and in the workplace by bringing women's concerns to the attention of policy makers through litigation and education. The center has worked to open the full range of military assignments to women and has advocated expanded protections against sexual harassment and sex-based discrimination in the military. The NWLC publishes numerous articles and issue papers concerning women in the military, including articles critical of antipregnancy policies at military colleges.

RAND Corporation
PO Box 2138, 1700 Main St., Santa Monica, CA 90407-2138
e-mail: correspondence@rand.org • Web site: www.rand.org

RAND, which stands for "research and development," is a think tank that provides research findings on a wide variety of subjects to policy makers. Its research on women in the military has concluded that women do not pose a threat to military readiness and that the opening of new opportunities for women has been successful. Its studies on women in the military include *New Opportunities for Military Women* and *Military Readiness: Women Are Not a Problem*. RAND also publishes the quarterly *RAND Review*.

Women's Research and Education Institute (WREI)
1750 New York Ave. NW, Suite 350, Washington, DC 20006
(202) 628-0444 • fax: (202) 628-0458
e-mail: wrei@wrei.org • Web site: www.wrei.org

The WREI provides information to government officials, women's advocates, and other groups on issues affecting women and their roles in the family and the workplace. Since 1989 the WREI has monitored the opportunities available to women in the military by gathering research data and disseminating the findings on its Web site. The WREI also publishes *Women in the Military: Where They Stand*, now in its third edition.

Bibliography

Books

Rick Bragg and Jessica Lynch — *I Am a Soldier, Too: The Jessica Lynch Story*. New York: Knopf, 2003.

Francine D'Amico and Laurie Weinstein, eds. — *Gender Camouflage: Women and the U.S. Military*. New York: New York University Press, 1999.

Gerard J. DeGroot and Corinna Peniston-Bird, eds. — *A Soldier and a Woman: Sexual Integration in the Military*. Harlow, UK: Longman, 2000.

Lorry M. Fenner and Marie E. deYoung — *Women in Combat: Civic Duty or Military Liability?* Washington, DC: Georgetown University Press, 2001.

Linda Bird Francke — *Ground Zero: The Gender Wars in the Military*. New York: Simon & Schuster, 1997.

Stephanie Gutmann — *The Kinder, Gentler Military: Can America's Gender-Neutral Fighting Force Still Win Wars?* New York: Scribner, 2000.

Margaret C. Harrell et al. — *The Status of Gender Integration in the Military*. Santa Monica, CA: RAND Corporation, 2002.

Melissa Herbert — *Camouflage Isn't Only for Combat: Gender, Sexuality, and Women in the Military*. New York: New York University Press, 1998.

Nancy Mace — *In the Company of Men*. New York: Simon & Schuster, 2001.

Brian Mitchell — *Women in the Military: Flirting with Disaster*. Washington, DC: Regnery, 1998.

T.S. Nelson — *For Love of Country: Confronting Rape and Sexual Harassment in the U.S. Military*. New York: Haworth Maltreatment and Trauma, 2002.

Rita James Simon, ed. — *Women in the Military*. New Brunswick, NJ: Transaction, 2000.

Rosemarie Skaine — *Women at War: Gender Issues of Americans in Combat*. Jefferson, NC: McFarland, 1999.

Judith Hicks Stiehm, ed. — *It's Our Military, Too!: Women and the U.S. Military*. Philadelphia: Temple University Press, 1996.

Laurie Weinstein and Christie C. White, eds. — *Wives and Warriors: Women and the Military in the United States and Canada*. Westport, CT: Bergin and Garvey, 1997.

Periodicals

Gregory Beals et al.	"'Get Out of My Way': Women Soldiers, Making Quiet Progress, Now Hold Dangerous Combat Positions," *Newsweek*, October 29, 2001.
J. Michael Brower	"A Case for Women Warfighters," *Military Review*, November/December 2002.
J. Michael Brower and Elaine Donnelly	"Symposium: Whether to Assign Servicewomen to Submarine Duty," *Insight on the News*, April 3, 2000.
Mona Charen	"Why Does the United States Put Its Mothers into Combat?" *Insight on the News*, April 29, 2003.
Christian Science Monitor	"New World Order: Co-ed Trenches. Germany Tuesday Became the Latest Nation to Let Women Join Combat Units," January 4, 2001.
Kim Field and John Nagl	"Combat Roles for Women: A Modest Proposal," *Parameters*, Summer 2001.
E.J. Graff	"Bring Me Women," *American Prospect*, May 2003.
Stephanie Gutmann	"Sex and the Soldier: The Road from Aberdeen," *New Republic*, February 24, 1997.
Christopher Hanson	"Women Warriors: How the Press Has Helped—and Hurt—in the Battle for Equality," *Columbia Journalism Review*, May/June 2002.
Scott Heller	"Laundry, Canned Goods, and Rape: A Scholar Explores the Military's Impact on Women," *Chronicle of Higher Education*, April 14, 2000.
Michael Janofsky and Diana Jean Schemo	"Women Recount Life as Cadets: Forced Sex, Fear, and Silent Rage," *New York Times*, March 6, 2003.
Nicholas D. Kristof	"A Woman's Place," *New York Times*, April 25, 2003.
Steven Myers	"A Woman Serving on the Blurred Edge of Combat," *New York Times*, March 19, 2003.
Kate O'Beirne	"A New Horror of War: What Kind of Country Sends Its Girls and Mothers into Combat?" *National Review*, April 21, 2003.
Blake Points and Anne M. Coughlin	"Women and the Military," *Iris: A Journal About Women*, Fall 2002.
Anna Quindlen	"Uncle Sam and Aunt Samantha," *Newsweek*, November 5, 2001.
Joan Ryan	"Women and Uncle Sam," *San Francisco Chronicle*, January 14, 2003.
Rowan Scarborough	"In War's Wake, No Further Combat Roles Seen for Women," *Washington Times*, June 23, 2003.
Deborah Simmons	"Fighting for the Real Rights of Women; Combat Should Be Restricted to Men," *Washington Times*, March 28, 2003.

Anna Simons	"Women Can Never 'Belong' in Combat," *Orbis*, Summer 2000.
Melvina Smith	"When Mom and Dad Are in the Military," *Parents Magazine*, May 2003.
John Solomon and Thomas McGuire	"A-Ten-Shun: It's Time to Register Women for the Draft," *Boston Globe*, January 28, 2001.
Cathy Booth Thomas	"Conduct Unbecoming: One Female Cadet's Tale in the Air Force Academy's Growing Rape Scandal," *Time*, March 10, 2003.

Index